Human&Nature

爱风的女孩
The Girl Who Loved the Wind

青闰 张创 译注

-第2版-

东华大学出版社·上海

图书在版编目 (CIP) 数据

爱风的女孩 / 青闰, 张创译注. — 2版. — 上海: 东华大学出版社, 2015.5
ISBN 978-7-5669-0767-7

I. ①爱… II. ①青… ②张… III. ①散文集—中国—当代 IV. ① I267

中国版本图书馆 CIP 数据核字（2015）第 074714 号

策　　划	法兰西论坛
责任编辑	沈　衡
封面设计	杨　军　潘志远

爱风的女孩
青闰　张创　译注

出版发行	东华大学出版社（上海市延安西路1882号, 200051）
本社网址	http://www.dhupress.net
淘 宝 店	http://dhupress.taobao.com
天猫旗舰店	http://dhdx.tmall.com
营销中心	021-62193056　62373056　62379558
投稿信箱	83808989@qq.com
印　　刷	苏州望电印刷有限公司
开　　本	787 mm × 960 mm　1/32
印　　张	10.125
印　　数	0 001~4 000
字　　数	230 千字
版　　次	2015 年 5 月第 2 版　2015 年 5 月第 1 次印刷
书　　号	ISBN 978-7-5669-0767-7/I・010
定　　价	22.00 元

编者的话

经过精心策划,我们隆重推出"人与自然系列丛书":《爱风的女孩》、《紫丁香的回忆》、《牛仔的梦想》、《燕鸥满天》、《午夜秋千》和《春天的承诺》共六本。

我们之所以把这个系列叫作"人与自然",是因为我们想在设定的特殊背景下,充分展现人与自然的融融亲情和相互间千丝万缕的联系,让读者朋友从中领略到一种源于自然、归于自然的感召力和神秘感。

这里有人与飞禽走兽、花草虫鱼的亲情友爱,有人与山川湖泊、日月星辰的息息相通,也有人征服自然的勇敢和机智,具有极强的亲合力和包容性。

我们这里所选译的文章长短不一,由易到难,循序渐进,逐步提高;它们的风格多彩多姿,或优美隽永,或汪洋恣肆,或科学严谨,或撼人心魄,或催人泪下,或励人心志,或生动有趣……可谓色彩缤纷,美不胜收。

为了帮助读者朋友准确快捷地领会原文、最大限度地汲取英语精华,本系列丛书采取英汉对照的形式进行编排,并对疑难词加注音标和词义。在翻译上,我们力求准确到位,再现原作神韵,使读者既能学到地道纯正的英语,又能管窥到汉语的博大精深。同时,我们还配制了精美贴切的情景图片，使您能赏心悦目、乐在其中。

  本书在翻译过程中得到了丹冰、慕容韵、云中君、常飞雁等教授的悉心指导，在此深表谢忱。

青 闰
2015 年 4 月

前 言

　　《爱风的女孩》是"人与自然系列丛书"的第一本，采用英汉对照和生词注解的方式编排。

　　本书共选译文章 26 篇，这些文章故事性强，文字简洁，原汁原味，情节引人入胜。

　　有人与鸟兽息息相通、亲情交融的：月光郊狼、又见四月天、小狼波波、爱琴海上的鹈鹕鸟、有羽毛的朋友、虎儿在我心、战马回乡；

　　有动物与动物相依相偎、亲密无间的：史朗的爱、对话海豚、考拉熊的新家、白尾鹿；

　　有自然和谐、甜蜜芬芳的：第一场落雪、春天的紫罗兰、彩虹一家亲、爱风的女孩；

　　有人类不畏风险征服自然的：黑骏马、飓风中的女孩、飞马火焰、跟着爷爷出海、坠入矿井、闯过沼泽的少女；

　　有机智勇敢、生动奇趣的：救生筏上的男孩、28 层楼上的小男孩、望海少年、苹果树下的太空飞船。

　　这些故事像一只只神奇灵动的手拨动着你的心弦，使你一睹为快、一读难忘，并从中呼吸到清新自然纯净的英语空气，轻松走上英语的第一级台阶。

青 闰
2015 年 4 月

Contents
目 录

The Coyotes in the Moonlight
2
月光郊狼
3

Another April
14
又见四月天
15

Shiro's Love
28
史朗的爱
29

The First Snowfall
34
第一场落雪
35

Black Horse
48
黑骏马
49

	The Wolfkin Bobo	62
	小狼波波	63
	The Boy on a Raft	72
	救生筏上的男孩	73
	The Girl in the Hurricane	84
	飓风中的女孩	85
	The Violets in Spring	96
	春天的紫罗兰	97
	The View from the 28th Floor	106
	28层楼上的小男孩	107
	The Pelicans above the Aegean Sea	116
	爱琴海上的鹈鹕鸟	117
	The Sea Watcher	130
	望海少年	131

	The Rainbow	142
	彩虹一家亲	143
	The Koalas' New Home	148
	考拉熊的新家	149
	The Whitetail	158
	白尾鹿	159
	The Talking Dolphin	168
	对话海豚	169
	Flying Blaze	174
	飞马火焰	175
	Spaceship under the Apple Tree	184
	苹果树下的太空飞船	185
	Grandpa at Sea	198
	跟着爷爷出海	199

	Feathered Friend	206
	有羽毛的朋友	207
	The Hunter and a Red Fox	222
	猎人与红狐	223
	Fallen in the Mine	228
	坠入矿井	229
	The Girl Who Loved the Wind	246
	爱风的女孩	247
	The Girl out of the Swamp	254
	闯出沼泽的少女	255
	We'll Remember, Tiger	276
	虎儿在我心	277
	Jumper Back Home	294
	战马回乡	295

The Coyotes in the Moonlight

Joe and I had just finished breakfast. We were having a last, slow cup of coffee. That's when we first saw the two coyotes[1].

They stood watching our lonely cabin. They must have smelled the meat we had cooked. Winter food was hard to find on the snowy plain. We felt sorry for them. Soft-hearted Joe wanted to feed them.

"Go ahead," I said. "throw them some meat. But I bet they won't take it. Ranchers[2] put out poisoned meat for coyotes. They learn not to trust food that's offered."

But Joe cut off two chunks[3] of meat and went outside.

At first the coyotes stood their ground[4]. Joe got about thirty yards from them. Then they became excited. They backed slowly into the bush. They were too scared to make a stand[5]. But they were too hungry to leave. Joe dropped the meat on the snow and started back to the cabin.

---

[1] coyote /kɔi'əuti; (US) 'kaiəut/ n. 郊狼
[2] rancher /'ræntʃə/ n. 牧场主
[3] chunk /tʃʌŋk/ n. 大块
[4] stand one's ground 不屈服；不让步
[5] make a stand 准备抵抗；摆开架势

月光郊狼

我和乔刚吃过早饭,正慢慢地喝着最后一杯咖啡。就是在那个时候,我们第一次看到了那两头郊狼。

它们站在那里望着我们孤零零的小木屋。它们一定是闻到了我们做饭的肉香。冬天在雪原上是很难找到食物的。我们为它们感到难过。软心肠的乔想给它们东西吃。

"去吧,"我说,"给它们扔些肉。但我敢说它们是不会吃的。牧场主们经常为郊狼放下过毒的肉。它们已学会了不相信主动送给它们的食物。"

但乔还是切了两大块肉,走了出去。

起初,那两只郊狼站在那里没有动。乔离它们大约有 30 码远。随后,它们跃跃欲试,慢慢地退回到了丛林里。它们太害怕不敢摆开架势,但它们又太饿不愿离开。乔将肉放在雪地上,然后返回了小木屋。

He was halfway back when coyotes raced to the meat. Each one snapped up[1] some and ran into the bush.

Joe and I had come to Wyoming to look for gold. We had found this old log cabin just as winter caught us. We were safe there from the cold north wind and the snow.

The cabin sat at the foot of a mountain. We could see all around us for miles. But there just wasn't much to do. It was so lonely and silent. We said that coyotes' howling[2] kept us company.

Until the sun came up, we would hear them. They would start with a few sharp yaps[3]. Then they got louder. Their song would always end in a long, sad howl.

Of all the wild animals that roam the Great Plains, I like coyotes best. It's easy to like these sly little wolves. You'll always hear them when the sun goes down on a winter day, singing to the land they love.

Joe and I were glad the two coyotes didn't forget us. They hunted on a trail down the river. Our cabin was near their trail. As they came by on the early morning, they always stopped.

---

[1] snap /snæp/ up 迅速抓取某物
[2] howl /haul/ n. 尖声嚎叫
[3] yap /jæp/ n. 吠叫

他刚走回半路上,两只郊狼就飞奔到了那两块肉旁边,各自飞快地叼起一块肉,跑进了丛林里。

我和乔来怀俄明州淘金。正当冬天来临之际,我们发现了这个旧木屋。在那里,我们可以免受寒冷的北风和雪的袭击。

小木屋坐落在一个山脚下。我们可以看到方圆几英里的物体,但没有多少事做。周围是那样孤独和寂静。我们常常说,郊狼的嗥叫声陪伴在我们左右。

太阳升起以前,我们常常听到它们的嗥叫声。它们开始叫时经常带着尖叫声,随后声音越来越响亮。它们的吠叫总是以一声悲怆的长嗥而结束。

在所有漫游在大平原的野生动物中,我最喜欢郊狼。喜欢上这些狡黠的小郊狼是很容易的事儿。当冬天的傍晚太阳落山时,你总是会听到它们对它们热爱的大地歌唱。

那两只郊狼没有忘记我们,这让我和乔感到很高兴。它们沿着河边的一条小路猎捕。我们的小木屋就在那条小路附近。它们早上路过时总是会停下来。

Like I said, that winter they had a hard time finding food. The small animals they hunted were safe in holes under the snow. The coyotes were thin under their heavy fur.

The male was a rather large coyote. Also, he was kind of[1] afraid. The female was small and brave. Whenever we saw them, she was in the lead[2]. He kept a few steps behind. Maybe she was too hungry to be afraid.

She had learned that we had no dogs around. She knew we wouldn't hurt her. As she came close to the cabin, though, the male would stay behind. About twenty yards from the door she would stop. That was the line she would not pass. She just trotted[3] back and forth until we opened the door.

Joe or I would go out with food. She would back up a little and wait. The male would go hide behind some bush. They waited until the cabin door closed. Then they would run for the food. And they would always share it!

Mostly the coyotes came to our cabin just after sunup. They often seemed tired. They had been hunting down by the river. When they were down there, they had to watch for poisoned food, guns, and traps.

One morning in March, our coyote friends failed to come.

---

[1] kind of （口）有点儿
[2] be in the lead /li:d/ 处于领先地位
[3] trot /trɔt/ vi. 小跑

像我所说的那样，那年冬天它们寻找食物非常艰难。它们要猎捕的那些小动物都安全地呆在冰雪覆盖的洞里。两只郊狼厚厚的皮毛下都瘦成了皮包骨头。

那只公狼个头很大，同时也有点儿胆怯。那只母狼个头很小，却很勇敢。无论我们什么时候看到它们，小母狼总是打头阵。公狼常常站在后面几步远处。也许是母狼太饿才不害怕的吧。

母狼已经得知我们周围没有狗，知道我们不会伤害它。然而，当母狼走近小木屋时，公狼总是留在后面。在离门大约20码处，母狼常常会停下来，通常不会越过那条线，只是前后小跑着，直到我们把门打开。

无论是乔还是我总是带着食物出来。母狼常常会后退一点，在那里等待着。公狼藏进某个灌木丛后面。一直等到小木屋门合上，它们才向那食物跑去。而且它们总是一起分享！

两只郊狼大都是在太阳刚刚升起之后来到我们小木屋边，好像总是非常疲惫。它们一直沿着河边捕猎。到那里时，它们不得不提防着下过毒的食物以及猎枪和陷阱。

三月的一天早上，我们的郊狼朋友没有来。

We were worried. All that day we looked toward the river. We kept hoping they would turn up. But evening came, and we hadn't seen them. Other coyotes howled that night. But our two friends didn't answer.

We went to the window many times the next morning. We were sure something ugly had happened. It was a cloudy, gray morning. The snow was nearly gone, and a sharp wind blew through the brush. We ate breakfast in silence. Joe was very sad. He had started the friendship with the coyotes. Now it seemed to have ended. The wind blew through and as I was staring out the window, something caught my eye.

"Look, Joe!" I cried. "You see what I see? Out there by that low rise?"

He ran to the door. "It's them!" he shouted. "Come on[1]!"

We ran out. I didn't even put on a cap. Our coyotes were struggling toward the cabin. We soon could see they both were worn out.

The little female was dragging a terrible steel trap. Its sharp jaws bit into one of her legs.

But still she was not alone. Her mate held the trap chain in his teeth. He had helped her pull the heavy thing through the brush.

---

[1] come on 用于祈使句，以鼓励某人做某事，尤指促其加速、努力或试一试

我们忧心忡忡，整整一天都在向河那边张望，一直希望它们会出现。但夜晚来临了，也没有看到它们。那天夜里其他的郊狼嗥叫着。但我们的两个郊狼朋友没有回音。

第二天早上，我们一次次地走到窗边，相信一定是发生了什么不幸的事。那是一个多云的、灰暗的早晨。雪融化殆尽，风呼啸着穿过灌木丛。我们默默地吃着早饭。乔非常伤心。他已经跟那两只郊狼建立起了友情。现在好像这种友情就要结束了。风吹过来，当我望着窗外时，某个东西引起了我的注意。

"看，乔！"我大声叫道，"你知道我看见了什么？在那个低洼的地方？"

乔跑到门口，大声叫道："是它们！快点儿！"

我们跑了出去。我甚至连帽子都没有戴。我们的郊狼正挣扎着朝小木屋走来。我们立即就看出它们俩已经筋疲力尽了。

小母狼拖着一个可怕的钢夹，钢夹的利齿咬进了它的一条腿。

但它不是孑然一身。它的同伴用牙咬着那个钢夹链，帮它拖着那个沉重的东西穿过了灌木丛。

Had they come to find us? We had been friendly. They were not afraid of us. Surely they knew we would help.

As we came near, they stopped. He backed away to hide behind a bush. But she stood and watched us. Her tired eyes were shining.

"She may snap at[1] you. Her leg looks real[2] bad," I warned Joe.

Joe stooped and took hold of her furry neck. Softly, he talked to her.

Then he said, "Get at[3] that trap now. I've got her even if she should act up[4]."

It must have hurt when I took off the trap. But the little coyote didn't do a thing.

We went back to the cabin. The two coyotes came along. The female was again in the lead. She limped on three legs. They ate the food we put out. Then they went away.

From then on we saw the coyotes less often. Spring had come and changed their wintertime habits. They were getting ready to start a new family.

Joe and I went back to work. We were looking for gold again. We used the cabin only for sleeping now. There was no snow, so we couldn't see coyote tracks.

---

[1] snap at 一下子咬住
[2] real /riːəl/ *ad.* （口）非常；的确
[3] get at 着手处理
[4] act up 耍脾气；捣蛋

它们是来找我们的吗？我们曾是好朋友。它们不害怕我们，知道我们肯定会帮助它们。

当我们走近时，它们停了下来。公狼向后退进了一个灌木丛。但母狼却站在那里望着我们，疲惫的眼睛闪闪发亮。

"它也许会咬你。它的腿看上去的确是受伤了，"我警告乔说。

乔弯下腰，抱住它毛茸茸的脖子，对它轻轻地说着话。

随后，他说："现在要着手处理掉那个夹子。就是它耍脾气，我也得那样做。"

当我取下那个夹子时，它一定很痛。但那只小郊狼没有丝毫的挣扎。

我们回到了小木屋。两只郊狼也跟了过来。母狼又一次走到了前面，三条腿一瘸一拐地跳着。它们吃着我们摆出来的食物，之后就走了。

从那以后，我们看到两只郊狼的次数就少了。春天已经来临，郊狼改变了它们冬天的习惯，它们正准备建立一个新家庭。

我和乔重新投入工作，再次寻找起了金子，现在只把那个小木屋当作睡觉的地方。因为没有雪，所以我们无法看到郊狼的踪迹。

The spring rains stopped. The brush all turned green. Then one night we heard a little cry at the door. I jumped out of the bed and looked outside. There in the moonlight stood our little coyote. She had something in her mouth.

At first I thought it was a rabbit. Then saw she was carrying a coyote pup.

She stepped into the cabin and carefully laid the pup on the floor.

Suddenly, Joe exclaimed, "It's hurt! Its paw is bleeding." He picked up the pup and looked at the paw. I went to get hot water. "It doesn't amount to anything. Looks like something fell on its paw," he said.

But the mother had brought the pup[1] to us. She wanted us to do something about it. So we did what

we could to help. While we cleaned the foot with soap and water, the mother didn't move. She just whined as if telling us to hurry up. She had remembered us. But it was time to go. Joe put the pup down on the floor. The mother picked it up in her mouth. She ran off in the silver moonlight.

---

[1] pup /pʌp/ *n.* 幼小动物

春雨停止。灌木丛都开始泛绿。后来有一天夜里，我们听到了门边传来微弱的叫声。我从床上跳起来，向门外望去，只见月光下站着我们的小郊狼，嘴里衔着一个什么东西。

起初我还以为那是一只兔子，后来才看到它是衔着一只小狼崽。

它走进了小木屋，小心翼翼地将小狼崽放在地上。

乔突然大声叫道："它受伤了！它的爪子还在流血。"他抱起那只狼崽，看着那只受伤的爪子。我过去端热水。"不要紧。看上去好像是什么东西掉在了它的爪子上。"他说。

但它的母亲将它送到了我们这里，想要我们对此做点儿什么。因此，我们就尽我们所能帮助它。在我们用肥皂和水清洗它的蹄子时，它的母亲一动不动，只是呜呜地叫着，好像是在催我们要快点。它还记得我们。到了该走的时候了，乔将小狼崽放在地上。它的母亲将它衔在嘴里，跑进了银色的月光中。

Another April

Mom put a heavy wool hat on Grandpa's head. "Now," she said. "You will not get cold. Wait until I get your gloves."

"Do not get them," Grandpa said. "My hands will not be cold." But Mom went to get the gloves. Grandpa and I looked at each other.

"Your mother is putting enough clothes on me to kill a man," Grandpa laughed. His rough[1] laugh was like a March wind among the treetops[2]. I started to laugh, too. He thought I was laughing at his words and he was pleased[3]. But I was laughing at his clothes.

Grandpa wore a heavy wool suit that hung from his shoulders. It was tight[4] around his middle where he was round and full. His thin legs were like sticks inside the pants.

Mom had dressed Grandpa as if there were snow on the ground, but there was not. April was here and the sun was shining on the green hills where trees were covered with flowers.

When I looked at Grandpa and then looked out the window at the sunshine and green grass, I laughed harder. Grandpa laughed with me.

---

[1] rough /rʌf/ *a.* 粗犷的
[2] treetop *n.* 树梢
[3] pleased /pli:zd/ *a.* 高兴的
[4] tight /tait/ *a.* 紧的；牢的

又见四月天

妈妈将一顶厚厚的羊毛毡帽戴到爷爷的头上说:"好了,这样你就不冷了。等一下,我给你拿手套。"

"别拿了,"爷爷说,"我的手不会冷的。"但妈妈还是去拿手套了。我和爷爷面面相对着。

"你妈妈给我穿这么多衣服,都快把我给捂死喽,"爷爷笑道。爷爷粗犷的笑声像树梢间的三月风一样。我也开始大笑起来。他以为我是因为他说的话可笑才笑的,所以他乐呵呵的。不过,我是笑他的衣服。

爷爷穿着厚厚的羊毛衣,肩上的衣服耷拉着,腹部滚圆,衣服撑得紧绷绷的,两条细腿像两根小棍悬在裤腿里。

妈妈让爷爷穿得很多,就像地上有雪似的,但并没下雪。已经是四月份了,阳光照耀着翠绿的小山,那里的树上鲜花朵朵。

我瞧了爷爷一眼,又望了望窗外的阳光和绿草,笑得更厉害了。爷爷也和我一起笑了起来。

"I am going to see my old friend," he said when Mom returned with his gloves.

"Who is he, Grandpa?" I asked. But he did not hear what I said. He just stood there as I did when I was younger and let Mom put the gloves on his hands.

"I am going to see him now." Grandpa said. "I know he will still be there waiting for me."

Mom opened the front door for Grandpa. He walked slowly outside, holding his strong wooden cane[1] in one hand. With the other hand he held on to the door. I wanted to go with him, but Mom would not let me go.

I wondered what he was going to do out there in the spring sunshine. Perhaps he would take off his shoes when he got far away from the house. That is what I did when Mom could not see me. Sometimes I put my feet into the cool water of the river. I wondered if Grandpa would do that.

I watched him as he slowly walked down the road in front of the house. Mom watched him too. I think she was afraid he would fall, but she was wrong. Grandpa walked along the road better than my baby brother could walk.

---

[1] cane /kein/ n. 拐杖

"我要去看一位老朋友,"当妈妈拿着手套回来时,他说。

"他是谁,爷爷?"我问,但他没听见。他只是站在那里,像我小时候那样让妈妈给他戴上了手套。

"现在我要去看他了,"爷爷说,"我知道他还在那里等我。"

妈妈替爷爷打开前门。他慢慢地走到外面,一只手拄着他那根结实的木手杖,另一只手扶住门。我想跟他一起去,但妈妈不让我去。

我想知道他要在春天的阳光下出去做些什么。也许他走得离房子远些时会脱下鞋。当妈妈看不见我时,我就常这样做。有时我把脚伸进凉爽的河水里。我不知道爷爷是否会这样做。

我目送着爷爷顺着门前的路慢腾腾地走。妈妈也在望着他。我想她是怕他摔倒,但她错了。爷爷可比我刚会走路的弟弟强。

"He used to[1] be a powerful[2] man," Mom said. "He could cut down trees. No man could cut down more trees than Grandpa. He could lift the heaviest tree in the woods."

"Who is Grandpa going to see?" I asked.

"He is not going to see anybody," she answered softly.

"I heard him say that he was going to an old friend," I told her.

Mom gently smoothed my hair. "Oh, he was just talking," she said.

I watched Grandpa stop under the pine tree in our front yard. He put his cane against the tree and pulled off his gloves. Then he slowly reached[3] down toward the grass. He picked up a spring flower. He broke it into little pieces as if he was looking for something. Then, he dropped the pieces on the ground.

"What is Grandpa doing?" I asked Mom, but she did not answer me. "How long has Grandpa been with us?" I asked her.

"Oh, he came before you were born," she said. "He has been with us eleven years. He stopped cutting down trees when he was eighty years old; now he is ninety-one."

---

[1] used /juːst/ to 过去经常
[2] powerful /ˈpauəful/ a. 强有力的
[3] reach /riːtʃ/ vi. 伸手

"他以前身体很壮,"妈妈说,"他能砍倒大树。没有人比爷爷砍得更多。他能举起树林里最重的树。"

"爷爷要去看谁?"我问。

"他谁也不看,"妈妈轻声答道。

"我听他说要去一位老朋友那里,"我告诉她。

妈妈温柔地捋了捋我的头发,说:"噢,他只是随口说说。"

我看到爷爷在我家前院的那棵松树下停下来。他将手杖靠在树上,脱下手套,慢慢地把手伸向草地,采起一朵春花,将花揉成碎片,好像在寻找什么东西。接着,他把碎片撒在地上。

"爷爷在干什么?"我问妈妈,但她没有回答我。"爷爷和我们在一起有多长时间了?"我又问她。

"噢,他是在你出生前来的,"她说,"和我们在一起生活11年了。他是80岁那年停止砍树的;现在他91岁了。"

Mom had told me many stories about Grandpa. He would go out and cut trees in the coldest winter days. Mom often told me how the water on his face would turn into ice—but he never felt cold.

Now Mom would not let him go out of the house in winter.

As I watched Grandpa go toward the farm animals, he stopped to look at every little thing along the road. Once he waved his cane at a bird that flew over his head. Sometimes he stood still and held his face up against the soft spring wind. He took off his hat and let the wind blow his white hair.

Grandpa called to the animals and they ran toward him. He reached down and he touched every animal.

This was the first time Mom had let Grandpa out of the house since last autumn. I knew that Grandpa loved the sunshine and the fresh April air that blew across the fields. He loved the insects, the animals, the trees and flowers. And every day, from spring until winter, Grandpa would take this little walk.

But each year his walk was shorter. This spring he did not go down to the farthest end of the farm as he did last year. I remembered Grandpa's first walks when he would go far away. In those years he walked from one end of the farm to the other. When he returned to the house, he would tell me about the things he had seen.

Now, Grandpa stayed near the house.

妈妈告诉过我好多有关爷爷的故事。在冬天最冷的日子里，他常常出去砍树。妈妈常常告诉我，他脸上的汗水是怎样结成冰的——但他从不感到冷。

现在妈妈不让他冬天出门了。

这时，爷爷向农场上的动物走去，只见他停下来留心看路上每一个细小的东西。一次，他向飞过头顶的小鸟挥了挥手杖。有时他会静静地站在那里，让脸迎着柔和的春风。他摘下帽子，让风吹拂他的白发。

爷爷向那些动物大声喊着，它们都跑向他。他弯下腰摸摸这个，又摸摸那个。

去年秋天以来，这是妈妈第一次让爷爷出门。我知道爷爷热爱阳光和吹过田野的四月的新鲜空气。他喜欢小虫子、动物和花草树木。从春天到秋天，爷爷每天都出去散一小会儿步。

但他散步的路程一年比一年短。今年春天，他没有像去年那样走到农场的最远处去。我还记得爷爷散步到很远的地方时的情景。那时候，他从农场这头走到那头。等回来时，他就把所见所闻讲给我听。

现在，爷爷只能逗留在房子附近。

My Mom and I watched Grandpa go down on his knees and looked closely at the ground, I wondered what he was looking at.

I heard him say: "There you are, my good old friend."

"Who is his friend, Mom?" I asked.

Mom did not say anything. Then I saw what it was. It looked like a flat stone, but it was a turtle. "He is playing with that old turtle, Mom." I said.

"I know he is," she answered in a soft voice.

"The turtle does not get angry when Grandpa touches him, does he?" I asked.

She shook her head.

"But that old turtle will not let me touch him," I said. "Why does he let Grandpa get near him?"

Mom smiled in a secret way. "The turtle knows your Grandpa," she said.

"He should know me, too," I said. "But when I come close he just hides inside his shell[1]."

Mom did not seem to hear me. She was listening to Grandpa talk to the turtle. "It has been a hard winter," Grandpa said to the turtle. "Did you suffer in your home underneath the barn[2]?" The turtle turned his face to one side. He was trying to talk to Grandpa. Perhaps the turtle could understand what Grandpa was saying.

---

[1] shell *n.* 龟壳
[2] barn *n.* 谷仓；牲口棚

我和妈妈看着爷爷双膝跪下来,贴在地上看。我不知道他在看什么。

我听到他说:"你在这里呀,我好心的老朋友。"

"谁是他的朋友,妈妈?"我问。

妈妈没有吭声。随后,我看到了那是什么。那东西看上去像是一块扁平的石头,其实是一只海龟。"他在和那只海龟玩,妈妈,"我说。

"我早就知道了,"她柔声答道。

"爷爷动它时,它不生气吗?"我问。

她摇了摇头。

"但那只老海龟是决不让我碰它的,"我说,"为什么它让爷爷接近呢?"

妈妈神秘地笑了笑,说:"海龟认识你爷爷。"

"它也应该认识我呀,"我说,"但我一靠近它,它就把头缩进了龟壳里。"

妈妈好像没有听我的话。她正在听爷爷跟海龟说话:"一冬天很冷,你在棚舍下的家里受罪吗?"海龟把脸扭向一边。它试图和爷爷说话。也许它能听懂爷爷在说什么。

"I am happy to see you again, old fellow," Grandpa said. The turtle sat quietly and let Grandpa's big hand touch him.

"I do not understand why the turtle does not bite him," I said.

"That turtle has lived under the barn for many years," Mom explained. "Grandpa has known him for eleven years. He talks to the turtle every spring."

"Is the turtle old like Grandpa?" I asked.

"Well, it has the number 1847 cut into his hard shell," Mom said. "He might be older than that."

Then I wondered how a turtle could get that old and what kind of person had cut the number on his back. I wondered where it happened—if it happened near our house. I wondered what sort of man lived here then, if he had cut down trees like Grandpa. I wondered if he enjoyed April as Grandpa always did. I wondered if he talked to this same turtle.

"Are you healthy, old fellow?" Grandpa asked the turtle. The turtle just looked back and closed his eyes.

"Did the turtle ask Grandpa if he was healthy?" I asked.

"I do not know," Mom said softly. "I cannot talk to turtles."

"But Grandpa can," I said proudly.

Grandpa was talking again. "Wait until the tomatoes get red," he promised the turtle, "and we will go into the garden together."

"很高兴又见到你,老伙计,"爷爷说。海龟静卧在那里,让爷爷的大手抚摸它。

"我不明白海龟为什么不咬他,"我说。

"那只海龟在棚舍下生活了很多年,"妈妈解释说,"爷爷认识它已经有 11 年了。每年春天,他都要和海龟说说话。"

"海龟和爷爷一样老吗?"我问。

"唔,它的硬壳上刻着 1847 这样的数字,"妈妈说,"它可能比那更老。"

接下来,我想知道海龟怎么能活这么久、是什么人在它背上刻下的数字。我想知道是在什么地方刻的,是不是在我家附近。我也想知道那时这里曾住过什么人、他是不是也和爷爷一样总是喜欢四月。我还想知道他是不是也总是和这只海龟说话。

"你身体还好吧,老伙计?"爷爷问海龟。海龟只是向后看了一眼,就合上了眼睛。

"海龟问过爷爷身体好吗?"我问。

"我不知道,"妈妈温柔地说,"我不会跟海龟说话。"

"但爷爷会,"我自豪地说。

爷爷又在说话了。"等到番茄红了,"他对海龟许诺说,"我们一起去菜园。"

This was another surprise for me. I did not know that turtles ate tomatoes.

"That turtle had been eating tomatoes from our garden for many years," Mom said. "He is almost like one of our family."

"Gee," I said, "Grandpa looks like the turtle, doesn't he?" Mom's eyes filled with tears and she tried to smile.

"I'll be back to see you," Grandpa said. "I am getting cold now, I must go back into the house." The turtle pushed his head out more to watch as Grandpa slowly moved away.

"Goodbye, old friend," he called.

The turtle watched Grandpa until he came into the house, then went back under the barn.

这又让我吃了一惊。我不知道海龟还会吃番茄。

"那只海龟吃我们家菜园的番茄已经有好多年了,"妈妈说,"它几乎就像我们家的一员。"

"哎呀,"我说,"爷爷看起来像那只海龟,对吗?"妈妈的眼里噙满了泪花,她努力露出了笑容。

"我会回来看你的,"爷爷说,"我现在渐渐冷了,我必须得回屋里去了。"当爷爷慢慢地离开时,海龟的头又伸出来张望。

"再见,老朋友,"他喊道。

海龟目送着爷爷,直到他走进屋里,它才又回到了棚舍下。

Shiro's Love

"Shiro! Shiro!"

Mr. And Mrs. Nakamura were worried.

Their dog Shiro was missing. "Shiro!" They called again and again. Mr. and Mrs. Nakamura lived on a small island in Japan. They looked everywhere on the island, but they didn't find Shiro.

The next day Mr. Nakamura heard a noise at the front door. He opened the door, and there was Shiro. Shiro was very wet, and he was shivering[1].

A few days later Shiro disappeared[2] again. He disappeared in the morning, and he came back late at night. When he came back, he was wet and shivering.

Shiro began to disappear often. He always disappeared in the morning and came back late at night. He was always wet when he came back.

Mr. Nakamura was curious. "Where does Shiro go?" he wondered. "Why is he wet when he comes back?"

---

[1] shiver /ˈʃivə/ vi. 颤抖；哆嗦
[2] disappear /ˌdisəˈpiə/ vi. 消失；失踪

史朗的爱

"史朗！史朗！"

中村夫妇非常担心。

他们家的狗史朗失踪了。"史朗！"他们喊了一遍又一遍。中村夫妇住在日本的一座小岛上。他们把岛上都找遍了，但没找到史朗。

第二天，中村先生听到前门响了一声，便打开门，发现史朗站在那里，浑身湿透，瑟瑟发抖。

几天后，史朗又一次失踪了。它早上失踪，夜里很晚才回来。它回来时，浑身精湿，抖个不停。

史朗开始经常失踪。它总是早上失踪，夜里很晚才回来。回来时，身上总是湿淋淋的。

中村先生感到非常好奇。"史朗到哪里去了呢？"他心里琢磨道，"它回来时身上为什么那么湿呢？"

One morning Mr. Nakamura followed Shiro. Shiro walked to the beach[1]. He ran into the water and began to swim. Mr. Nakamura jumped into his boat and followed his dog. Shiro swam for about two miles. Then he was tired, so he climbed onto a rock and rested. A few minutes later he jumped back into the water and continued swimming.

Shiro swam for three hours. Then he arrived at an island. He walked onto the beach, shook the water off, and walked toward town. Mr. Nakamura followed him. Shiro walked to a house. A dog was waiting in front of the house. Shiro ran to the dog, and the two dogs began to play. The dog's name was Marilyn. Marilyn was Shiro's girlfriend.

Marilyn lived on Zamami, another Japanese island. Shiro and the Nakamuras used to[2] live on Zamami. Then, in the summer of 1996, they moved to Aka, a smaller island. Shiro missed Marilyn very much and wanted to be with her. But Shiro wanted to be with the Nakamuras, too. So, Shiro lived with the Nakamuras on the island of Aka and swam to Zamami to visit Marilyn.

---

[1] beach /biːtʃ/ n. 海滩
[2] used /juːst/ to 过去经常

一天早上，中村先生尾随着史朗。史朗走到海滩。它跑进水里，开始游泳。中村先生跳上他的小船，跟随着他的狗。史朗游了大约两英里。随后，它累了，便爬到一块岩石上休息。几分钟后，它又跳进水里，继续游了起来。

史朗游了三个小时。随后，它来到一座岛上。它走到海滩上，将身上的水抖落，然后向城里走去。中村先生在后面跟着它。史朗向一所房子走去。一只狗正在房前等着。史朗跑到那条狗身边。随后，两条狗开始玩了起来。那条狗的名字叫玛丽琳。玛丽琳是史朗的女友。

玛丽琳住在日本的另一座岛——座间味岛上。史朗和中村一家曾经住在座间味岛上。后来，1996年夏天，他们搬到了一座更小的岛——赤井岛上。史朗非常想念玛丽琳，想和她呆在一块。但史朗也想和中村一家呆在一块。所以，史朗就和中村一家住在赤井岛上，然后游到座间味岛去看望玛丽琳。

People were amazed¹ when they heard about Shiro. The distance from Aka to Zamami is two and a half miles. The ocean between the islands is very rough². "Nobody can swim from Aka to Zamami!" the people said.

Shiro became famous. Many people went to Zamami because they wanted to see Shiro. During one Japanese holiday, 3000 people visited Zamami. They waited on the beach for Shiro. "Maybe Shiro will swim to Zamami today," they said. They all wanted to see Shiro, the dog who was in love.

---

[1] amazed /əˈmeizd/   *a.* 强调"使惊异、困惑",间或还有"惊叹、佩服"的意思,是意义很强的词。
[2] rough /rʌf/   *a.* 汹涌的;狂暴的

  人们听说了史朗的事，感到非常吃惊。从赤井岛到座间味岛有两英里半。两座岛之间的海水非常凶猛。"谁也不能从赤井岛游到座间味岛！"人们说。

  史朗一下子出了名。好多人去座间味岛，因为他们想看到史朗。在日本的某个假日，3000人来到了座间味岛上。他们在海滩上等候史朗。"也许史朗今天会游到座间味岛呢，"他们说。他们都想见见史朗——那条正在恋爱的狗。

The First Snowfall

The snow kept coming down, quietly, covering the land deeper and deeper. It seemed as if it would go on forever. It was the first snowfall of the year.

Bill looked through the kitchen window, lost in the whiteness outside. He felt like[1] diving[2] into the snow and burying himself in its softness.

"Billy," his mother shouted. She was standing at his side, but had to raise her voice because he was not listening.

"Do you have to call me Billy?"

"I meant Bill," his mother answered quickly. "I forgot how close you are to being a man. Go help Pa with the fence."

Bill started out toward the fence. That was the foot story of his life[3]…fixing this, fixing that.

He walked slowly. The falling snow had a strange power…it was like magic. Billy wanted to keep going, wishing there was no fence to fix.

And then suddenly, out across the fields he went. He did not know what he was doing.

He liked to help his father, but he kept thinking that at home he would never be more than a boy with small jobs to do. And working with Pa was not much fun. Pa did not talk much.

---

[1] feel like 想要
[2] dive /daiv/ *vi.* 下潜
[3] the foot story of one's life 表示某人生活(经历)的缩影

第一场落雪

雪在不停地下着,悄无声息,将地面覆盖得越来越厚。好像要永远持续下去一般。这是今年下的第一场雪。

比尔透过厨房窗户往外看,沉迷在外面的皑皑白雪之中。他真想一头扎进雪里,将自己埋进那柔柔的白雪。

"比利,"他母亲喊道。她正站在他的身边,但不得不提高声音,因为他没在听。

"你非得叫我比利不可吗?"

"我是说比尔,"他母亲飞快地回答道,"我忘记你离男子汉不远了。去帮你爸爸扎篱笆吧。"

比尔朝篱笆走去,那就是他生活的缩影……修这修那。

他慢腾腾地走着。落下的雪有一种莫名其妙的力量……就像魔术一样。比利想继续这样走下去,希望走到没有篱笆可修的地方。

随后,他突然越过田地,走了出去。但他不知道自己要做什么。

他喜欢给父亲做帮手,但他一直在想,在家里他决不仅仅是个干小活的男孩。再说,和爸爸在一块干活没有多少乐趣,他是个少言寡语的人。

He crossed the frozen creek, and then walked up into the hills. When he came down into the flatlands[1], he began to run, racing[2] against the whole world.

Then, he saw his friend Joey, standing near his father's barn, with a pail[3] in his hand.

"What's got into you?" Joey asked.

"I just feel good, that's all."

"You look kind of funny," Joey said.

Billy wiped his hot face with snow.

Joey said he was going to the Town Hall for music and dancing, and Billy went with him.

The Town Hall was on a hill between two long valleys[4]. As they drove up, they heard music coming out of the Hall.

Joey tied the sled and horses. Billy looked out over the east valley. All he could see was white through white: the low white hills through the snowflakes[5].

"Come on," Joey called to him. "You'll catch cold standing out there."

Inside the Hall, the air was sweet and warm. Some of the girls smiled at Billy in a funny way. He could not tell if the smiles were friendly or not.

---

[1] flatland n. （复数）平原地区
[2] race vi. 飞奔
[3] pail n. 桶
[4] valley /'væli/ n. 山谷
[5] snowflake /'snəufleik/ n. 雪花

他穿过冰冻的小溪，随后走上小山。下到平地时，他开始奔跑，与世界赛跑。

随后，他看到了朋友乔伊，乔伊手里提着桶正站在他父亲的谷仓附近。

"你怎么了？"乔伊问。

"我只是感觉不错，仅此而已。"

"你看上去有点儿可笑，"乔伊说。

比利用雪抹了一把热辣辣的脸。

乔伊说，他要去镇里的音乐厅听音乐和跳舞。比利和他就一块儿去了。

镇里的音乐厅位于两个长山谷之间的一座小山上。他们滑上去时，听到音乐从大厅里传出来。

乔伊拴好马和雪橇。比利朝东边的山谷望去。他所能看到的就是白茫茫的一片：透过雪花看到了低低的、白白的小山。

"快点儿，"乔伊对他喊道，"你站在那里会感冒的。"

大厅里的空气甜蜜而温馨。一些女孩对比利古怪地一笑。他无法说出那笑容是否友好。

He turned back to the door and decided to stand there for a moment and then go. There was too much noise inside.

"You are standing right in a drift[1]," someone said to him. It was one of Joey's cousins, Sheila something-or-other[2]. She lived in the next town. Billy didn't even know her last name.

"Oh," he said, his face getting red; he moved a little.

"You're still in it," she said.

Billy looked at her. She was sort of[3] pretty, with long black hair, blue-green eyes. But Billy wished she would go away. "It's only fresh air," he said. "Go pick on[4] somebody else."

"I'm not picking on you, I'm trying to help you, that's what."

"Too many think they're helping when they're not, do you?"

She studied[5] him. "Well," she said, "that's true."

Then she smiled. "You don't like it in here, do you?"

"I feel better outside."

---

[1] drift *n.* 雪堆
[2] something-or-other 别的什么
[3] sort of *ad.* 有几分
[4] pick on 选中
[5] study *vt.* 端详;打量

他折回到门口,决定在那里站一会儿再走。里边太吵了。

"你站在风口,"有人对他说。那是乔伊的一个表妹,叫希拉什么的。她住在邻近的镇上。比利甚至不知道她姓什么。

"噢,"他说,脸变得通红;他往边上挪了一点儿。

"你还在风口,"她说。

比利看着她。她还算漂亮,长长的黑发,碧蓝的眼睛。但比利希望她走开。"只有这里空气新鲜,"他说,"去找别人吧。"

"我不是要找你,我是想帮你,仅此而已。"

"许多人并不是帮忙时,却认为自己是在帮忙,对吗?"

她打量着他。"噢,"她说,"说的对。"

随后,她笑了起来。"你不喜欢这里,对吗?"

"在外边感觉更好。"

"It's snow...I saw you through the window, just before you came in. I feel that way myself about a first snow."

Without thinking, Billy said, "Look, would you like to go out...just for a few minutes?"

She turned her head away, and then said, "I'll get my coat."

Outside, they stood in the snow looking at the lighted windows of the Hall. She walked quietly beside him. He could still hear the music from the Hall, but it was part of the snowfall.

It seemed strange and wonderful that there should be someone so near him.

Suddenly he asked, "Did you say something?"

"No," she said. "did you?"

He shook his head.

"What do you think about when you walk like this?" she asked.

"Oh, different things...what I'd like to do and never can...it's daydreaming[1], I guess."

"Yes," she said. "I do that too."

The snow seemed to be falling faster now, and the music from the Hall was gone. From far below came the sound of bells, followed by a few coughs from an old car...then there was just silence, as if the snow had cut off all the sounds of the world. Billy looked at her white coat and hat. They belonged to that world of wonder, that world of magic that was born with the first snowfall. He touched her hat.

---

[1] daydream /ˈdeidriːm/ *vi.* 做白日梦

"外面在下雪……你进来前,我透过窗户看见了你。第一场雪给我的感觉就是那样的。"

比利不假思索,说道:"喂,你想出去吗……就几分钟?"

她扭过头,然后说:"我去拿大衣。"

到了外面,他们站在雪中望着大厅灯光照耀的窗户。她静静地走在他的身边。他仍能听到从大厅里传出来的音乐,但那已经成了这场雪的一部分。

有人离他如此之近,是那样妙不可言。

突然,他问道:"你说过什么吗?"

"没有,"她说,"你说过吗?"

他摇了摇头。

"你现在想什么呢?"她问。

"噢,是截然不同的事儿……是我想做但却从来不能做的事儿……我想是白日梦。"

"是的,"她说,"我也是那样想的。"

现在雪似乎下得更快了,而且大厅里的音乐已经听不见了。远处山下传来了钟声,随后传来了一辆旧车发动机发出的声音……接下来是寂静,好像雪已经将世界上所有的声音切断了似的。比利看着她的白大衣和白帽子。它们属于那个神奇世界,那个伴随第一场雪而来的神秘世界。他抚摸着她的帽子。

"What are you doing?"

"I don't know," he said. "I just..." He stopped. There was nothing real but the snow. Even the whiteness[1] of her coat and hat seemed to come from the snow.

He turned around. All signs of the road were gone. "We are the only two in the world left," he said.

"Is that why you touched my hat?"

He said nothing...but then bravely he said, "Maybe I wanted to kiss you."

She laughed. "I wouldn't let you," she said.

"Why not?"

"I'm too strong for you," she said.

"So that's what you think...you're wrong. If I really wanted to, I guess I could do it, all right."

"Dreamer[2]..." She gave him a push, and ran back toward the Hall.

Before he knew it, he was after her. He had caught her. Laughing, she pushed him and down they went into the snow.

He expected her to let him kiss her now. That's what often happened in the stories he read. Why would she laugh if her struggle against him were real? But she did not let him.

"You're a child," she said, pulling away from him.

---

[1] whiteness / '(h)waitnis/ n. 此处指雪
[2] dreamer n. 梦想者

"你在做什么?"

"我不知道,"他说,"我只是……"他停了下来。除了雪,什么都不是真实的。甚至她的大衣和帽子上的白色也似乎是从雪上来的。

他转过身。所有的道路都消失了。"世上就剩我们两个人了,"他说。

"这就是你摸我的帽子的原因吧?"

他什么也没说……但随后,他勇敢地说:"也许我想吻你一下。"

她笑出了声。"我不会让你吻的,"她说。

"为什么不能?"

"我对你来说太强大了,"她说。

"你是这样想的……那你就错了。我要是真想亲你,我想我是能做到的,肯定能。"

"做梦……"她推了他一下,然后回头向大厅跑去。

还没等他明白过来,他就向她追去。他追上了她。她笑着推了他一下,他们都倒进了雪里。

他希望她现在让他吻她。这在他看过的小说中是经常发生的。她要是真的反抗,为什么要笑呢?但她就是不让他吻。

"你还是个孩子,"她想要挣脱。

I should let go, he thought. But he held on to her, until he felt that he could hold on[1] forever…he wanted to hold forever. It was really a simple thing to hug a girl, he thought.

Her hat had been pushed off, and the snow shone on her dark hair. He now felt a strange gentleness for her.

The snow was light and cool as a fresh white sheet, but still he held on.

Very gently, Billy kissed her a third time. Then, he let her go and they stood up. He picked up her hat and put it on her head. They began to walk back toward the Hall, and the music come to them again, as light as the snow that had covered them.

As they walked, her hand touched his. She didn't mean to do it. Her touch was just another part of what now seemed to be a world of light and gentle things.

"Do you want to go back in the Hall?" she asked. Her voice was low…she no longer looked so strong.

"I guess not," he answered. "Are you going in?"

"I'd better," she answered, "I came with friends. I'll see you again, won't I?"

---

[1] hold on 坚持住

我应该放手,他心想。但他紧紧地抱住她,直到他感到他能永远地抱下去……他想永远地抱下去。拥抱一个女孩真是一件简单事儿,他心想。

她的帽子被推开,雪落在了她的黑发上,亮晶晶的。他现在对她有一种莫名其妙的温柔。

雪像白色的新床单一样清爽,但他仍紧紧地抱着。

比利非常温柔地第三次吻了她,随后便放开了她。他们站了起来。他拾起她的帽子,戴在她的头上。他们开始回头向大厅走去,音乐又在他们耳边响起,就像落在他们身上的雪一样轻。

他们一边走,她的手一边摸着他的手。她似乎是不经意的。现在,她的抚摸就像轻柔世界的另一部分。

"你想回到大厅里边吗?"她问。她的声音很低……她看上去不再那么强大了。

"我不想,"他回答说,"你进去吗?"

"我最好还是进吧,"她回答说,"我是和朋友们一块儿来的。我还会见到你的,不是吗?"

Her question surprised[1] him. He had not thought about seeing her again. He was still lost in a dream, thinking of the day's happening, feeling the wonder and excitement of newborn things, like the first snowfall, the first spring flowers, the first feelings of growing up, becoming a man.

Billy heard her ask again. "I'll see you again, won't I?"

He shook his head.

"You mean I won't?" she said.

"I mean you will," he answered.

She smiled and went inside. He began walking along the road toward the valley.

---

[1] surprise /sə'praiz/ *vt.* 使吃惊

她的问题使他吃了一惊。他没想过再见她。他仍沉迷在梦里,想着这天所发生的事儿,感受到新生事物的神奇和激动,就像第一场落雪、第一束春花、长大成人后的第一次感觉。

比利听到她又问道:"我会再见到你,难道不是吗?"

他摇了摇头。

"你是说我不会再见到你了?"她问。

"我是说你会的,"他答道。

她微微一笑,走了进去。他开始沿着大路向山谷走去。

Black Horse

Jed got to the top of the mountain and sat down to rest. The July sun had made him hot. It had been a long walk to the top and he was tired. He knew the horse he was trying to capture[1] could not be too far away. He looked at the mountain and the valleys[2] below, searching footmarks[3] left by the horse.

Then he saw the marks going down the other side of the mountain. He must capture the horse. He knew better men than he had tried. Tom Raglan, the best rancher[4] in the state, had tried with the help of his cowboys. But they had not been able to capture it. It had gotten away from others, too. They all said it was too wild. It could not be captured.

After a slow, painful walk down the mountain, Jed came to a cool-looking river. He drank the clear water. Further down the valley he saw the black horse. It stood under a tree out of the sun. Jed moved closer, then hid behind a tree to watch. It was the biggest and blackest he had ever seen.

---

[1] capture /ˈkæptʃə(r)/ vt. 捕获；俘获
[2] valley /ˈvæli/ n. 山谷；溪谷
[3] footmark /ˈfutmɑːk/ n. 足迹
[4] rancher /ˈrɑːntʃə(r)/ n. 大牧场主

黑骏马

杰德到达山顶,就坐下来休息。七月的太阳使他热汗淋淋。他走了很长一段路才到达山顶,所以感到浑身乏力。他知道他想方设法要逮住的那匹马离此处不会太远。他察看着山上及下面的山谷,寻找着那匹马留下的蹄印。

这时,他看到在山的另一侧,顺坡而下有一行马蹄印。他一定要逮住那匹马。他知道曾有比他更有能耐的人试过。州内最好的牧场主汤姆·拉格伦就曾经在他那帮牛仔的帮助下尝试过,但他们并没能逮住那匹马。其他试图去逮它的人也都让它逃脱了。他们都说它太野,是不可能被逮住的。

顺着山路向下,慢慢地、艰难地走了一段后,杰德到达一条看上去十分清澈的河边,喝了几口河水。接着又沿山谷向前走了一段,这时他看到了那匹黑马。它站在一棵树下遮太阳。杰德又走近了些,然后躲在一棵树后观察。这是他有生以来见过的最大、最黑的马。

Jed knew all about horses. He had grown into a man caring for them. He had never earned more than $10 but he had dreams: If he could get a male and female horse and 10 hectares[1] of land, he could sell horses. That would be all the happiness Jed wanted.

Night came. The big black horse moved from under the tree and began to eat grass near the river. Jed watched again. A few hours later, he found a soft place in the ground. He placed his head against an old fallen tree and slept.

The next day he woke with the sun. His eyes searched for the horse, and there it was, grazing. Jed saw how it ate, then lifted its head and looked all around. It was the mark of the wild, always looking for hidden danger.

Jed started to walk toward the horse. The horse stopped eating and looking at Jed. Jed's heart began to beat heavily. Men had said the horse was a killer. Still, he walked closer. Fifteen meters away from the horse Jed stopped. The horse had lifted its front feet high in the air, then placed them heavily back on the ground. Jed moved closer. He talked to the horse in a soft voice. Then, with a loud scream, the horse turned and ran down the valley. Jed sank to the ground wet with excitement. He had done what no man had done. He had almost touched the wild horse. The animal was not a killer. If it had been, Jed would be dead now.

---

[1] hectare /ˈhektɑː(r)/ n. 公顷

杰德对马了如指掌。他是个从小与马厮混、在马背上长大的人。尽管他挣的钱从来没超过10美元,但他有自己的梦想:如果他能得到一匹公马、一匹母马和10公顷土地,他就可以养马并以卖马为生了。那就是他想要得到的全部幸福了。

夜幕降临。那匹大黑马从树下走了出来,走到河边开始吃草。杰德继续观察着。几小时后,他在地里找了一块柔软的地方,将头靠在一棵倒着的老树上睡着了。

第二天日出时,他醒了过来,马上就去寻找那匹马,还好,它就站在那里,正吃着草呢。杰德看着它吃草,随后又见它抬起头,朝四周看了看。这就是野马的特征:它们总是十分小心,不时地看看四周是否有什么暗藏的危险。

杰德开始慢慢向它走近。它停止吃草,看着杰德。杰德的心开始咚咚直跳。人们都说这马是个杀手。但他还是继续向它靠近。在离它15米远的地方,杰德停了下来。只见它高高地抬起前蹄,然后又重重落回原地。杰德又走近了些。他开始柔声跟它说话。接着,随着一声响亮的嘶鸣,这匹马转身顺着山谷跑了下去。杰德却因兴奋而浑身大汗淋漓,倒在了地上。他已经做了别人没有做到的事儿,几乎快要挨到这匹野马了。它并不是个杀手。如果它是的话,杰德现在已经没命了。

For six days he followed the horse. He rested when the horse rested. Jed did not like the land they were in now. The sides of the valley were high and filled with big rocks. Few trees were around. And the bottom of the valley was soft and wet.

Jed watched the horse a while, and then lay down to sleep.

In the middle of the night, he was awakened by thunder[1] and rain. He walked up the rocks until he found a dry hole, safe from the rain, and he slept again.

The next day was cold and wet. Heavy rains had softened the bottom of the valley. He followed the horse most of the day. The wet valley was the only place it could walk now. The sides of the valley had gotten higher. Toward evening he saw it again. But this time there was fear in its face. He stopped and watched. The horse's nose was smelling the air. It smelled danger.

Jed thought of wild animals, a wildcat or bear maybe. He pulled his knife from his pants[2]. He looked among the rocks but saw nothing. He began walking toward the horse. The wildcat could have been on either side of the valley. He walked slowly, trying to watch both sides at the same time. Slowly he came to the horse's side. Jed kept watching the rocks. If the cat was going to attack[3], it would do it now. He felt the excitement of danger.

---

[1] thunder /ˈθʌndə(r)/ n. 雷声
[2] pants /pænts/ n.(pl.) 长裤
[3] attack /əˈtæk/ vt. 袭击；攻击

他一连跟踪了这匹马六天。只有马歇时，他才歇。杰德不喜欢他们现在所呆的地方。这山谷的两侧都很高，到处是大岩石。周围没有多少树。而且谷底又软又湿。

杰德观察了一会儿马，随后躺下来睡觉。

半夜时分，他被雷雨声惊醒。他立刻沿着岩石向上走，直到找了一个躲雨的干燥山洞，他才接着睡。

第二天又冷又湿。大雨已经泡软了谷底的土壤。这一天的大部分时间他都在跟着马走。湿湿的山谷是它现在唯一可以行走的地方了。越走，山谷两侧就显得越高。临近黄昏时分，他才又看见了它，但这一次它的脸上出现了一种恐惧的神情。他停下来仔细观察，只见马鼻子在嗅着空气。它闻到了危险的气息。

杰德想到是不是有什么野兽，一只豹猫，也可能是一只熊。他从裤子里抽出刀，在岩石间四处搜寻，但什么也没看见。他开始向马走过去。豹猫可能在山谷的某一侧。他走得很慢，尽力同时看着两侧。慢慢地，他来到了马身边。杰德一直盯着那些岩石。豹猫如果要袭击，它现在就会跳出来的。他感到既危险又兴奋。

Suddenly the silence was broken. The black horse screamed loudly, a cry of fear. It began running down the wet valley. At the same time there was a heavy, deep noise from the rocks. Then it happened. Tons of wet earth and big rocks began moving down the sides of the mountain. The land itself was the enemy.

When the air became clear, Jed looked for the horse. In front of him were tons of the fallen earth. He could not see down the valley and could not see the horse. He slowly climbed over the fallen rocks. On the other side was the horse, more frightened[1] than ever. Its legs were struck[2] in the soft earth and it could not move. The more it struggled, the deeper it sank in the mud[3].

Jed walked toward the animal. Each step he took, the soft mud tried to suck him down, too. He walked on the grassy places harder than the mud.

When he got to the horse, it was in the mud up to his stomach. Now it could move only its head. Jed felt wildly happy when he touched the horse. "Do not struggle and do not worry, Horse! I'll get you out!"

---

[1] frightened /'fraɪt(ə)nd/ *a.* 惊恐的
[2] strike *vt.* 使处于特定状态
[3] mud /mʌd/ *n.* 稀泥;烂泥

突然,寂静被打破了。黑骏马大声嘶叫起来,那是一种充满恐惧的叫喊。随后,它顺着湿漉漉的山谷奔跑起来。与此同时,岩石中传出了一种巨大而低沉的响声。紧接着,山洪就爆发了。成吨成吨的湿土和大岩石开始从山坡两侧滚落下来。原来山地本身就是马的敌人。

当空气恢复清新时,杰德立刻开始找马。在他面前是滚落下来的成吨的落土,他无法看到山谷的前方,也看不到马。他慢慢地爬过那些落下来的岩石。马在这个石土堆的另一边,看上去比先前更加恐惧。它的腿陷入了软土里,动弹不得。它越是挣扎,就在泥土中陷得越深。

杰德向它走过去。他每走一步都感到软泥也在将他往下吸,而且在长草的地方走比在泥里走还要艰难。

当他赶到马身边时,泥土已经没过了马肚子。现在它只剩下头部还能动弹。摸到马,他感到欣喜若狂。"别挣扎,别担心,马儿!我会把你弄出来的。"

Suddenly he felt the horse's teeth on his arm. He bit his lip to stop it from crying aloud. His free hand gently[1] calmed the horse and slowly it let go. It pressed[2] its nose against Jed's face. At last they were friends.

Now Jed could go to work. He studied the problem carefully. He had no way to lift the big horse from the mud. Certainly his rope was not strong enough. He began to pull the mud away with his hands. But more mud fell into the hole he dug. He ran to the rocks that had fallen down the mountain. He took off his shirt and filled it with rocks. He dug again. Only this time, he placed rocks in the holes he dug. The rocks stayed still and slowly a wall began to form. He did this through the day and when night came, his hands were bloody, torn by the sharp rocks.

He knew night would be a bad time for the horse. He did not want it to become frightened and struggle against the wall of rock he was building in the mud. He cut some small trees, laid them on the ground next to the horse and all through the night, he spoke soft, kind words to it to calm its fears.

The next morning, he brought grass for it to eat and began his work again. It was slow, hard work. When night came, he lay next to the horse again. He did not want it to struggle yet. The time had not come for the test.

---

[1] gently /'dʒentli/ *ad.* 和蔼地；温柔地
[2] press *vt.* 压；推

突然，他感到马的牙齿咬住了他的手臂。他咬住嘴唇，以防自己疼得叫出声来。他用那只没被咬着的手轻抚马身，使它平静下来，慢慢地让它松开了嘴。随后，马将鼻子贴在了杰德的脸上。最后，他们成了朋友。

现在杰德可以开始忙活了。他仔细研究了这个问题。他没有办法将这么大的马从泥里拽出来，他的绳子显然不够结实。他开始用手将泥刨开，但这样做后，更多的泥又落进了他刚挖开的窟窿里。他就跑到那些山上落下的岩石边，脱下衬衣将岩石裹住，又挖了起来。这一次，他将岩石放进了他挖开的窟窿里。岩石稳稳地呆在里面，慢慢地形成了一面挡土石壁。他整整挖了一天。夜幕降临时，他的两手已经被尖锐的岩石划得血淋淋的。

他知道，夜晚对马来说是难熬的。他不想让马害怕，以至于挣扎起来踢坏了他在泥里建好的石壁。他砍了一些小树，将它们放在马旁边的地上。另外，整整一夜，他都跟马说着温柔友善的话以消除它的恐惧。

第二天早上，他抱来些草让它吃，然后又开始忙活起来。这是一项耗时而又艰苦的工作。夜幕降临时，他又在马旁边躺了下来。现在他还不想让马从泥中挣扎出来，考验的时刻还没到。

By the middle of the next day, he had enough rocks in the mud on one side of the horse. Now he began to dig near the horse's front legs. His rocks began to make the mud harder. The horse was able to move a little. And when the pressure became less, it raised one of its front legs on to the rocks. It pushed against the rocks on its side and lifted its body a little out of the mud.

Jed got his rope and tied it around the horse's neck. He began to pull on the rope. The horse felt the pull and struggled with all its power against the mud. It raised its other front leg on the rocks and with a mighty[1] push with its back legs and with Jed pulling on its neck, it moved forward toward hard land. Jed fell on the earth, happy but tired. He had not eaten for three days. He had slept little. Half sleep, he felt the horse's nose push against his face. He jumped to his feet and when he brought grass for the horse it made friendly noises and playfully[2] pushed him.

A week later, a big black horse rode on the land owned by Tom Raglan. It stopped near the ranch house. A little man got off the horse's back. Tom Raglan looked at the horse with eyes that did not believe. Finally he said: "You got him."

"I got him, Tom, and I brought him back as I said I would."

---

[1] mighty /'maiti/ *a.* 强大的；强有力的
[2] playfully /'pleifuli/ *ad.* 爱玩耍地；嬉戏地

到第三天中午时,他在马一侧的泥里放进了足够的岩石。现在他开始挖马前腿附近的土。他放的岩石使泥坚硬了起来。马开始能动一点儿了。而感到压力变小了时,马将它的一条前腿拔了出来,翘到了岩石的上面,然后朝身边的岩石猛蹬,使它的身体从泥里稍微抬起了点儿。

杰德拿出绳子,将它系到了马的脖子上,开始拉绳。马感到了拉力,就用尽全力在泥里向外挣扎。马将另一条前腿也拔出来,搭在了岩石上,靠着后腿的巨大蹬力和杰德对它脖子施加的压力,它向前面的硬地移动着。杰德倒在地上,高兴而又疲惫。他已经三天没吃东西了,睡得也不多。正有点儿迷迷糊糊的,他感到马的鼻子拱到了他的脸上,他赶快一跃而起。当他为马抱来草料时,马发出了友好的叫声,顽皮地拱拱他,和他戏耍。

一周之后,有人骑了一匹大黑马来到汤姆·拉格伦的领地上。它在牧场房边停下来,一名小个子男人从马背上跳了下来。汤姆·拉格伦用吃惊的眼光看着这匹马,眼前的情景简直令他难以置信。最后,他说:"你得到了它。"

"我得到了它,汤姆,而且正我像我说过的那样,我把它骑回来了。"

Raglan looked at the horse. Above all, he was a horseman and there was no need for Jed to tell him how he captured it. Jed's tired face, his torn hands, dirty clothes and thin body told the story.

"Jed," Raglan said. "that horse will kill anyone except you. I do not want it. But I have not forgotten my promise. I will give you some land and the old house in back of the ranch if you will keep the horse there. I pay you $30 a month, if you will let me send my female horses to the black horse. I want the black horse's blood in my horses. And you can keep every seventh horse for yourself."

Jed put his arm around the black horse. The black horse was his. His dream had come true. It was too much all at once.

拉格伦看着马。他毕竟是个马主,没必要让杰德告诉他是怎么逮住马的。杰德疲惫的脸、划烂的手、肮脏的衣服和瘦弱的身体就已经说明了一切。

"杰德,"拉格伦说,"那匹马会弄死除你之外的任何人,我不想要它。但我没忘记自己的诺言。如果你让这匹马一直呆在这里,我就把一些土地和牧场后边的那座老房子送给你。如果你让我把我的母马送到你的大黑马那里去交配的话,我会每个月付给你30美元。我想要我的马的身体里都有大黑马的血统。而且,你可以留下交配后产下的小马中的七分之一。"

杰德伸出手臂,抱住大黑马。大黑马成他的了。他的梦想已经成为现实了。突然之间,他得到的真是太多了。

The Wolfkin Bobo

I first saw Bobo in a parking lot[1] in downtown[2] Vancouver, a city in western Canada. He was the most magnificent[3] wolf I had ever seen. The eyes were large and clear, the head was white and silver. He lay in a box in the back of a station wagon[4].

Bobo was three years old, and he was being sold by a person who had wanted to put him in the movies. But Bobo was too nervous[5] for movie work.

Looking at Bobo, I thought for a moment I must be crazy to buy him. I had a wife and two small daughters. What if my family were hurt?

---

[1] parking lot   n. 停车场
[2] downtown /ˈdauntaun/   a. 闹市区的
[3] magnificent /mægˈnifisnt/   a. 壮观的；气派的
[4] station wagon   n. （美）旅行车；客货两用车
[5] nervous /ˈnəːvəs/   a. 紧张不安的

小狼波波

　　我第一次看到波波是在加拿大西部城市温哥华闹市区的一个停车场。它是我曾见过的最有气派的狼。眼睛大而清亮，头部雪白，泛着银光。它躺在一辆旅行车的后备箱里。

　　波波才三岁，它是被一个想将它拍进电影的人卖掉的。但波波对电影拍摄感到非常不安。

　　看着波波，一时间我认为自己一定是疯了才买下了它。我有妻子和两个小女儿。如果我的家人受到伤害怎么办？

I hated to see Bobo without his freedom, but I could not let him run away. When I got him home, I put one end of a long chain on Bobo's neck, the other end to a tree near the girl's playhouse[1]. The next day Bobo seemed glad to see me. His tail wagged[2], and he bent his head low, exposing his throat. Bobo thought I was the leader of the pack[3]—never mind[4] the pack that was made up of four people and one wolf.

I had been told that when a wolf attacks, there isn't any defense. To fight back[5] is to invite death. If Bobo attacked, the only way to be alive would be to give up. I would have to stand with my arms around my throat, to bow my head and seem to be weak.

---

[1] playhouse /ˈpleɪhaus/ n. 娱乐室
[2] wag vt. 摇
[3] pack n. 群
[4] never mind 没关系；不用担心；不要紧
[5] fight back 反击；回击

我不喜欢看到波波失去自由，但我又不能让它跑走。当我将它带到家时，我将波波的脖子套在了一条长链上，另一端拴在了女儿的娱乐室附近的一棵树上。第二天，波波好像很高兴看到我。它摇摆着尾巴，将头垂得很低，露出了喉咙。波波以为我是一群中的头头——千万不要介意这个群体是由四个人和一头狼组成的。

我曾被告知，当一头狼进攻时，是没有任何防御措施的。要回击就意味着自取灭亡。如果波波进攻，惟一要活下来的方法就是放弃。我不得不把两臂护在自己的喉咙上，低下头，看起来非常虚弱。

I was frightened when I walked into the playhouse. I had a sleeping bag on my shoulder and a bag of meat. Bobo snapped[1] the meat from my hand, then he tore the sleeping bag from my shoulders and pulled it apart in seconds. Then Bobo jumped back to me, put his front paws on my shaking shoulders and licked my face. Bobo stood as tall and weighed as much I did. My leg became bent under me, and I fell backward. Bobo was on top, and we were wrestling[2] playfully. He could have killed me many times over, but his jaws remained closed.

For a full year, I spent at least six hours a day with Bobo. I began to see the difference between dogs and wolves. Most dogs like the company[3] of people and eager to please. Wolves with people hardly show a desire to please. If they are not the leader, they are not powerful in a group.

I knew that my family would have to live by pack law if they were to get along with Bobo. My daughter Sorrel was nearly three and Kester was not quite two. It was dangerous to have them around Bobo, but I believed that Bobo saw the girls as young wolves.

---

[1] snap /snæp/　*vt.* 攫取
[2] wrestle /ˈres(ə)l/　*vi.* 摔跤
[3] company /ˈkʌmpəni/　*n.* 陪伴

走进娱乐室时,我感到非常害怕。我的肩膀上有一个睡袋和一包肉。波波从我的手里夺走了肉,然后从我的肩膀上拽走了睡袋,不到几秒钟就把它撕成了两半。随后,波波又跳回我的身边,将前爪搭在我颤抖的肩膀上,舔着我的脸。波波站起来和我一样高,和我一样重。我的腿开始弯曲,然后我向后倒去。波波爬在了我的身上,我们在一块嬉戏扭打着。许多次它本来可以咬死我,但它的爪子始终没有张开。

在整整一年的时间里,我每天都要和波波在一起至少度过六小时。我开始明白了狗和狼的不同。大多数狗都喜欢与人为伴,渴望取悦。和人在一起的狼几乎不会露出取悦的欲望。如果它们不是头头,它们在狼群中就不会有影响力。

我知道,如果我的家人要和波波在一起相处,他们将不得不靠狼群的法则生活。我的女儿索莱尔才三岁,凯斯特还不到两岁。让她们在波波的身边是非常危险的,但我相信波波将两个小女孩看成了小狼娃。

Reading up on the feeding habits of wolves, I discovered that pack leaders generally[1] eat first. Only then can the other wolves eat. When there is plenty to eat or when young wolves are too young to hunt, they eat with their parents.

I set up a picnic[2] table near Bobo's chain. Bobo's meat would be in the middle of the table, and each of us would spread saliva[3] on the meat as though we had eaten of it. Then we would all walk to Bobo and offer him the meat.

After a while, I allowed the girl to turn the meat over to Bobo. Soon I let the girls lick their hands and offer them to Bobo. He would sniff gently, his nose trembling and his tongue caressing[4] their hands wetly. The girls would laugh as Bobo placed a front paw on top of their heads. Soon the girls were able to treat Bobo as a big playmate[5].

---

[1] generally /ˈdʒenərəli/ *ad.* 通常；一般地
[2] picnic /ˈpiknik/ *n.* 野餐
[3] saliva /səˈlaivə/ *n.* 唾液
[4] caress /kəˈres/ *vt.* 爱抚
[5] playmate /ˈpleimeɪt/ *n.* 玩伴

研究了狼吃东西的习惯之后，我发现狼群的头头一般先吃。只有头头吃过，其他狼才能吃。当吃的东西很多或幼狼太小还不能捕猎时，它们就和父母一块吃。

我在波波的链条旁边放了一张野餐桌。波波的肉通常放在桌子中央。我们每个人都在上面沾点唾沫，好像我们已经吃过了一样。随后，我们常常会都走到波波的身边，送给它肉吃。

过了一会儿，我让女儿把肉给波波翻过来，随后让女儿舔她们的手，然后递给波波。它会轻轻地嗅嗅，鼻子颤抖，舌头舔湿她们的手。当波波将前爪搭在两个女儿的头上时，常常她们会哈哈大笑。不久，两个女儿就能把波波当作是一个大玩伴了。

Learning to live by wolf law has had many moments of joy, but that joy often fills me with sadness. Sometimes at night I hear his call echo[1] like a lone, wild bell. At those times, I wonder by what right I chose to uproot[2] him from the wilds. There is no way back for Bobo. He can never live with a wolf pack now. But he shares his wolf heritage[3] with us, and for that we are thankful.

---

[1] echo /ˈekəu/   vi. 回响；回荡
[2] uproot /ʌpˈruːt/   vt. 迫使…离开出生地或定居地
[3] heritage /ˈheritidʒ/   n. 秉性

　学会和狼在一起生活的法则尽管有很多乐趣,但那种乐趣通常让我感到很忧伤。有时夜里我会听到波波叫唤的回声,就像孤独的旷野钟声一样。每当此时,我就想着我有什么权利迫使它离开荒野。没有办法让波波回去了。它现在再也不能和狼群生活在一起了。但它和我们一块分享了狼生活的传统,我们也为此而感激它。

The Boy on a Raft

The raft[1] was six feet long and three feet wide, and there were three of us on it. The engineer, with his head badly cut, and myself and Jack Keeley. Jack was a little boy from a poor family in London.

The little life raft certainly wasn't comfortable, but it was better than the sinking ship we had to leave. If a ship sinks in 30 minutes, you don't wait to see if a life raft is comfortable.

The first one on the raft was the engineer, who was thrown up onto it by a wave. I came later, after the ship had sunk. Then we heard Jack's voice. After a short time, we saw him perhaps 60 feet away and brought him aboard[2]. He had been holding on to a little piece of wood. He had on two life jackets[3] but very few clothes. He was so cold that his teeth were chattering[4] but he was very much alive.

On the night when the Benares sank, a cold wind blew from the north. The sea was rough[5], and the rain turned to ice as it fell. Once in a while the rain would stop for a few minutes, and we could see the moon.

---

[1] raft /ræft; rɑːft; (US) ræft/ *n.* 木筏
[2] aboard /əˈbɔːd/ *ad.* 上船
[3] life jacket *n.* 救生衣
[4] chatter /ˈtʃætə/ *vi.* 格格打战
[5] rough /rʌf/ *a.* 汹涌的

救生筏上的男孩

救生筏长 6 英尺、宽 3 英尺，上面坐着我们三个人。头部严重划伤的轮机师、我自己和杰克·基雷。杰克是伦敦一个穷人家的小男孩。

尽管小小的救生筏肯定不舒服，但总比我们不得不离开的将要沉没的轮船好。如果轮船将在 30 分钟后沉没，你就不会等着看一只救生筏是不是舒服了。

第一个上救生筏的是轮机师，他是被一个大浪甩上去的。轮船沉没后，我也爬了上来。随后，我们就听到了杰克的声音。过了一小会儿，我们看到了大约在 60 英尺外的他，就把他拉上了救生筏。他一直在紧紧地抓着一小块木头。他穿着两件救生衣，但贴身的衣服不多。他非常冷，所以牙齿格格打战，但他活得好好的。

在贝奈尔号沉没的那个夜里，一股寒流从北方吹了过来。波涛汹涌，雨下着下着就变成了冰。偶尔雨会停几分钟，随后我们看到了月亮。

Our ship was attacked at 10 o'clock at night. On board the Benares were 406 people, and 100 of them were children, all in bed. Twenty-four hours later 161—including 19 children—had been saved. The rest[1] were dead.

If you ever have to get someone onto a raft, and try to do it from the raft itself, the raft will turn over. To get Jack onto our raft, I had to drop into the water and push him aboard. While I was wondering how to get back myself without turning over[2] the raft, Jack said something I shall never forget. On his hands and knees, his teeth chattering, he looked down at me from the raft. "I say," he said. "I say…"

"Well?" I asked, thinking he might have a friend somewhere who ought to be saved.

"I say," he said, "thank you very much."

One wave in 50 broke over the top. We knew that because we counted the waves the next day when there was nothing else to do. And the waves came up through the spaces between the boards.

In a rough sea like that, one of us was always sliding off the raft. Jack was so little that he had great difficulty in staying aboard. So, through the night, we lay on top of [3]him. That kept a little of the cold wind from him, too.

---

[1] rest *n.* （前面与 the 连用）剩余
[2] turn over 翻转
[3] on top of 在…上面

我们的轮船是夜里 10 点受到袭击的。贝奈尔号船上有 406 人，其中 100 人是孩子，都躺在被窝里。24 小时后，161 人——其中包括 19 个孩子——已经得救。其他人都葬身大海。

如果你不得不把某个人弄到救生筏上，并尽力从救生筏上来做这件事，那么救生筏会翻过个来。为了把杰克拉上救生筏，我不得不跳进水里，将他推上救生筏。当我想着如何不弄翻救生筏而回到上面时，杰克说了一句我永远也不会忘记的话。他趴在那里，两手和膝盖着地，牙齿格格打战，从救生筏上向下望着我说："真的，我说……"

"说什么？"我问，想着他可能是在某个地方有一个应该救上来的朋友。

"真的，"他说，"非常感谢你。"

这时，50 个大浪中的一个掀过了筏顶。我们之所以知道，是因为第二天没什么事可做时就数起了那些浪。那些大浪是通过木板间的空隙进来的。

在像这样的汹涌大海中，我们当中的某个人总是会从救生筏上滑下去。杰克是那样小，所以呆在救生筏上极难。因此，那一夜，我们躺在他上方，那样也可以帮他挡住一点寒风。

There were cans of food on board, in a tidy little box fastened[1] at one side. There was even a can opener. But did you ever try to open a can with one hand while sitting on a raft in the middle of the Atlantic with 20-foot waves hitting you? If we set anything down on the raft, we risked its being swept away. That is how we lost one of our four cans of milk.

The only time we talked very much was just after one of these canned "meals." There isn't much to talk about on a raft in the Atlantic. There is, in fact, only one subject—and that is the subject you don't talk about.

Jack, however, did talk about it. After his breakfast of milk and hard bread, he asked questions which were difficult to answer. "I say," he demanded[2], "which way are we going?"

"Well," I said, pointing, "we're probably going that way. You see, the wind will blow us along."

"Yes," he said, patiently, "but which way? Are we going to the Untied States or are we going back to England?"

No, there isn't much to talk about—or much to do, either, in such a sea. Every half hour or so we would have to move ourselves about a little, because one of us was always about to slide into the water.

---

[1] fasten /'fɑːs(ə)n; (US) fæsn/ vt. 绑；系
[2] demand /dɪ'mɑːnd/ vt. 询问；查问

救生筏上有几罐食品,放在绑于一边的一只整洁的小箱子里。甚至还有起子。但当大西洋20英尺高的大浪袭击着你时,你能坐在救生筏上面用一只手设法打开食品盒吗?如果我们将任何东西在救生筏上放下,我们就可能会被冲走。我们就是这样失去四罐牛奶中的一罐。

我们惟一的聊天时间就是在吃过一罐罐装"饭"之后。在大西洋的一只救生筏上是不会有太多事可谈的。事实上,那里只有一个话题——而且那是你不想谈论的话题。

然而,杰克真的谈了。他吃过牛奶和硬面包早饭后,问了些难以回答的问题。"我说,"他问道,"我们是向哪个方向走呀?"

"噢,"我指着一个方向说,"我们也许是朝着那个方向走吧。你看,风吹着我们向前走呢。"

"是的,"他耐心地说,"但是哪个方向呢?我们是去美国还是返回英国呢?"

不,没有太多的话要谈——在这样的海上也没有太多的事可做。每隔半小时左右,我们就不得不稍微移动一点,因为我们其中一个人总是要滑进水里。

About noon, when it was warm, Jack and I tried to keep busy by counting the number of sea birds that were flying over our heads. Then Jack went to sleep and I sat looking at the horizon, thinking every little cloud might be smoke from a ship. But there was no ship. Not any other raft. No longer were there any pieces of the wrecked[1] ship. That was a long, long day. But Jack never once complained.

To keep warm, we moved our hands and arms and feet and legs. We twisted[2] and turned. We rubbed Jack. The more we could find to do, the less time we had for thinking about our troubles. But, as hope disappeared, a coldness came over us that not even the sun could drive away. We got careless about keeping close together[3]. We just lay there and thought and dreamed.

The engineer must have fainted. It had happened so quickly that to this day I do not know how it happened.

Jack pulled at me. "Look at him," he cried, "look!" I turned around to find the engineer sliding[4] off the raft. If he had gone, I don't think we could have brought him back again. Little by little[5], however, Jack and I pulled him back on the raft.

---

[1] wrecked /rekid/ a. 遇难的；失事的
[2] twist vi. 快速转动；旋转
[3] keep close together 呆在一起
[4] slide /slaid/ vi. 滑行；滑动
[5] little by little 渐渐地

大约中午时分，当天气暖和时，我和杰克就忙着数飞翔在我们头顶的海鸟的数量。随后，杰克就睡着了；我坐在那里看着地平线，想着每一个小小的云彩都可能是轮船上升起的烟。但没有轮船。也没别的救生筏。不再有沉没轮船的任何碎片。那是漫长的一天。但杰克没有埋怨过一次。

为了保暖，我们活动着双手、两臂、两只脚和两条腿。我们快速翻转着，摩挲着杰克。别的事情做得越多，想麻烦的时间就越少。但当希望消失时，一阵寒意向我们袭来，甚至太阳也无法将它驱走。渐渐地，我们对呆在一块儿心不在焉，只是躺在那里，想着，梦着。

那个轮机师一定是晕倒了。一切发生得是那样快，所以至今我都不知道究竟是怎么回事。

杰克拉着我。"瞧他，"他大声叫道，"快看！"我转过身，发现轮机师正从救生筏上滑下去。我现在仍然认为，如果他当时真的滑下去了，我们是不可能将他拽回来的。然而，我和杰克又慢慢地把他拉回到了救生筏上。

Then we thought of a new way of lying on the raft with our arms and legs twisted together around one another.

This woke Jack up completely. He talked rapidly about this and that for a time. Then he asked me another of his very difficult questions.

"I say," he asked, "I say, how do you stop these things when you want to get off?"

How? And when?

Heavy clouds were coming up to meet the setting sun. No more sea birds flew near us. The wind was stronger and the waves were even higher. There would be more of the rain that turned to ice. I decided we could have no more milk that day, we were down to our last can.

When the warship hooted[1], I didn't even look up. I had been hearing too many ships hooting all day, especially as night began to fall. I knew that they were only the sound of the waves beating against the raft.

The engineer, however, sat up. And slowly I understood. If two people heard a noise, maybe —

It seemed like hours before we rode up on a wave high enough to let us see the ship. And she was going away from us! Like dogs tied up and left behind in an empty yard, we shouted and cried and shouted again. Of course they couldn't hear us — we knew that.

---

[1] hoot /huːt; hut/ *vi.* 鸣响

随后,我们想到了一个新招,就是让彼此的胳膊和腿绞在一起躺在救生筏上。

这使杰克完全醒过来了。一时间,他飞快地谈这说那,随后问了我另一个非常难答的问题。

"喂,"他问,"我说,你是怎样不让自己滑下去的呢?"

怎样?什么时候?

乌云涌上来迎接着夕阳。不再有海鸟在我们附近飞翔。风力逐渐增大,海浪越来越高。将会有更多的雨变成冰。我心里想着,我们今天可能不会再有牛奶了,我们只剩下最后一罐了。

当那艘战舰响起时,我甚至连头都没有抬。我一天到晚一直听到轮船的鸣叫太多了,尤其是夜晚降临之时。我知道他们只是海浪撞击救生筏的声音。

然而,那个轮机师坐了起来。慢慢地,我明白了。如果是两个人听到了一个声音,也许——

好像过了好几个小时,我们才跃上一个高浪,看到那艘轮船。而那艘轮船正在远离我们!我们像被捆住扔在一个空院子里的狗一样,一遍又一遍地喊叫着。他们当然听不见我们的声音——这,我们知道。

We didn't know that they had already seen us and were sailing on a little farther to look at something that might have been another raft.

Suddenly the ship turned around and came toward us. The waves broke over her. Immediately we were calm and no longer cold. The ship came slowly up to us. A rope was thrown, but we could not catch it. Another hit me in the face, and we held on to that one.

Carefully, we lifted Jack to his feet. He couldn't stand, but, as the raft rose almost up to the deck on a wave, they caught him, and the engineer and I were in the sea again. Getting onto a ship in the middle of the ocean is much more difficult than getting off it!

Inside the steaming engine room, a sailor pulled our clothes off. Another appeared with hot milk for Jack and rum for me. The engineer was taken off to bed. Jack and I sat holding hands and smiling foolishly.

"Try a little of this," I said, putting a drop or two of rum into what was left of his milk. He drank it down.

"I say," he said, "I say, thank you very much."

Jack still couldn't stop his teeth from chattering. But he didn't cry. He didn't talk about home or about his sister. Later we learned that she had gone down with the Benares. He didn't complain.

He had saved his own life by his good sense, and he had saved the life of the engineer. He never once gave up hope. He returned cheerfully to London. Not bad — for a kid of eight. Jack Keeley, I am certainly pleased to have met you.

我们不知道他们已经看见了我们，他们是想再向前走一点，看那个可能是另一艘救生筏。

突然，那艘轮船转过头，向我们驶来。海浪在轮船上方劈裂开来。我们马上安静了下来，不再感到冷了。轮船慢慢地靠近了我们。一条绳子扔了过来，但我们无法接住。另一条绳子扔到了我面前，随后我们紧紧地抓住了那条绳子。

我们小心翼翼地将杰克拉起来。但他站不起来了，当救生筏几乎在一个大浪中跃上轮船甲板时，他们抓住了他。我和轮机师又落入了海中。在海里爬上一艘轮船要比下船难得多！

在一个蒸汽机房里，一名海员将我们的衣服脱了下来。另一名船员给杰克端来了热奶，然后向我跑来。轮机师被送到了床上。我和杰克紧紧地拉着手，坐在那里傻笑着。

"喝点儿这个，"我将一两滴朗姆酒放进了他剩下的牛奶中说。他喝了下去。

"真的，"他说，"真的，非常感谢你。"

杰克仍禁不住牙齿打颤。但他没有哭，没有谈他的家，也没有谈他的姐姐。之后，我们得知她已经随着贝奈尔号走了。他没有抱怨。

他凭着好运气救了自己一命，而且救了那个轮机师一命。他从来也没有放弃过希望。他兴高采烈地回到了伦敦。对一个 8 岁的男孩来说，真不错。杰克·基雷，我非常高兴曾和他相遇。

The Girl in the Hurricane

Henry was washing the kitchen floor for his mother. That was his job every Saturday.

He had the windows wide open. It was beginning to rain and the rain was beginning to blow. Henry was glad of that. The air had been so still and hot all day that he felt as if something heavy were pushing down on him.

"Hey, Henry! Look!" his younger sister Carol cried, running into the kitchen. "It's getting good and[1] windy outside."

Henry saw the kitchen curtains flapping[2] in the high wind.

"Good," Henry said, mopping in a corner. "It's getting cooler."

"I'm going out in the wind!" Carol said. "I'm going to park."

Henry looked outside again. "You are not," he said. "It's starting to rain."

"So what?" Carol said. "I'll wear my raincoat, and I'll come back if it rains hard. I promise."

"No," Henry said. "Just straighten up[3] your room or something and let me finish this floor. When this old floor is done, maybe we'll go out together."

---

[1] good and 非常
[2] flap *vi.* 摆动；拍动
[3] straighten /ˈstreitn/ up 整理；使整洁

飓风中的女孩

亨利正在为他的母亲拖洗厨房的地板。这是他每周六的工作。

他让所有的窗户都大开着。天开始下起了雨,而且雨越来越大。亨利为此感到高兴。整整一天空气凝固了,热得要命,他感到就像有一块什么东西压在他身上。

"嗨,亨利!瞧!"他的妹妹卡罗尔喊着,跑进了厨房。"外面的风好大。"

亨利看到厨房的那些窗帘在大风中摆动着。

"好,"亨利一边在一个墙角拖着地,一边说,"天越来越凉了。"

"我要出去兜风!"卡罗尔说,"我要去公园。"

亨利又看了看外面,说:"你不要去,下雨了。"

"那又怎么样?"卡罗尔说,"我会穿雨衣的,再说雨要是下大,我会回来的。我保证。"

"不要去了,"亨利说,"把你的房间整理一下,让我把地板拖完。等拖完这旧地板,也许我们可以一块出去。"

Carol went on talking. "I have straightened up my room. Mom knows how I like to skate in the wind. She lets me go alone. She really does."

Carol stopped talking only long enough to put on her raincoat, get her skates, and rush to the door.

"I'll come back if it rains hard," she called from the door. "I promise."

"Hey!" cried Henry, throwing down the mop[1] and running after her.

But Carol was already down the stairs and at the front door. "Mom always lets me," she called back. "She really does! So long!"

Henry frowned. Then he went back to the kitchen and picked up the mop again.

"If Mom lets her go, I guess I don't have to stop her," he said to himself.

Henry closed the window when the wind began to blow a little harder.

Then he looked at the clock and saw that it was time for his favorite music. He turned on the radio and listened as he mopped. The music was so loud that Henry didn't hear the wind blowing harder and whistling around the house. He didn't see the rain begin to stream down the window.

Suddenly the music stopped.

A voice on the radio said:

---

[1] mop *n.* 拖布

卡罗尔继续说着:"我已经整理过自己的房间了。妈妈知道我喜欢在风中滑冰。她让我一个人出去。她真的让。"

卡罗尔不再说话,只是用足够长的时间穿上雨衣、带上冰鞋,然后就冲到了门口。

"雨要是下大,我会回来的,"她从门口大声说道,"我发誓。"

"嘿!"亨利大声叫着,扔下拖布,向她追去。

但是,卡罗尔已经下了楼梯,跑到了前门。"妈妈总是让我这样,"她回头大声说道,"她真的会让我去!再见!"

亨利皱了皱眉,随后走回厨房,又拿起了拖布。

"要是妈妈让她去,我想我不必去拦她,"他自言自语道。

风开始刮得大了一点,亨利关上了窗户。

之后,他看了看钟表,发现已经到了他最喜欢的音乐时间。他打开收音机,一边拖地一边听着。音乐声很大,亨利没有听到风刮得越来越猛,在房子四周呼啸着。他也没有注意到雨水顺着窗户倾泻而下。

音乐突然停止。

收音机里传来一个声音:

"This is a special weather report. Hurricane will bypass[1] Springfield. But strong winds and heavy rains have hit the city and will keep up for several hours."

Hurricane! Henry turned pale.

The voice went on but Henry didn't hear it. He threw down the mop.

"Wow!" he said out loud. "How foolish can I get? There's a big storm outside. And I let Carol go out in it!"

He ran to get his raincoat and hat and hurried down the stairs.

He could hardly open the front door. The wind was blowing against the door so hard that it was like a strong man pushing against it, but at last Henry squeezed through[2]. When he was outside on the sidewalk, the wind hit him and he almost fell.

An empty garbage can blew over and crashed against the wall of a house, and the top of the can went rolling noisily into the street. The wind made a high, shrill[3] sound.

He must find Carol!

Henry began to run. He felt as if the wind and the rain were blowing him down the street. Which way should he go? He decided to head for the park where Carol had said she was going skating.

---

[1] bypass /'baipɑ:s; (US) 'baipæs/ vt. 绕过；绕…走
[2] squeeze /skwi:z/ through 穿过
[3] shrill a. 尖声的；伴有尖声的；充满尖声的

"现在是特别天气报道。飓风将要绕过斯普林菲尔德市,但强风和大雨已经袭击了我市,而且将持续好几个小时。"

飓风!亨利顿时变得脸色苍白。

广播员的声音继续着,但亨利已经听不到了。他扔下拖布。

"哇唔!"他大声说道,"我怎么能这样愚蠢?外面这么大的暴风雨。我却让卡罗尔跑了出去!"

他跑去拿雨衣和帽子,然后匆匆跑下楼梯。

他几乎打不开前门。风猛烈地吹着门,就像一个身强力壮的人在推着一般,但最终亨利还是挤了出去。当他到了外面的人行道上时,风向他袭来,差点儿把他刮倒。

一只空垃圾筒被刮倒,撞在了一堵墙上,随后垃圾筒顶轰隆隆滚进了街道。风发出了尖锐的呼啸声。

他一定得找到卡罗尔!

亨利开始奔跑起来。他感到风雨好像是在将他吹过大街。他应该走哪一条路呢?他决定去公园,卡罗尔说过她要去那里滑冰。

Just as Henry ran around the corner he heard a terrible crash and looked back. A huge grocery store sign had blown down.

Henry ran faster. Carol could really get hurt in this storm. He must save her.

On he went. The wind was blowing even harder now. It was growing dark. Twice he fell down. The four blocks seemed like a terrible endless dream.

At last he saw the little park ahead. The trees shook in the wind. Some broken branches trailed[1] in the grass.

"Henry!" a voice called.

"Carol!" he cried. "Is that you?"

"I'm over here. Holding onto the fence," she said.

Fighting the wind, Henry pushed his way over to the fence. And there was Carol, her skates over her shoulder, hanging on.

"I couldn't get home," she cried. "The wind kept blowing me down."

"You're all right now," Henry said, putting his arm around her. "Hang on to[2] me. I'll get you home."

---

[1] trail *vi.* 下垂
[2] hang on to 紧紧抓住

正当亨利跑过街角时,他听到了一声可怕的撞击声。他回头一看,只见一块巨大的百货店招牌被刮倒在地。

亨利跑得越来越快。卡罗尔可能真的会在这场暴风雨中受伤。他一定要救她。

他继续跑了起来。风现在刮得甚至更猛了。天越来越暗。他先后摔倒了两次。四个街区好像成了一场没有尽头的恶梦。

最后,他总算看到了前面的那个小公园:树在风中摇晃着,一些断裂的树枝垂落到了草丛里。

"亨利!"一个声音叫道。

"卡罗尔!"他大声喊道,"是你吗?"

"我在这里,在栅栏边上,"她说。

亨利顶风而行,一路飞奔到了栅栏边。卡罗尔站在那里,她的冰鞋挂在肩上,紧紧地抱着栅栏。

"我回不了家了,"她哭道,"风总是把我吹倒。"

"你现在没事儿了,"亨利一只胳膊抱住她说。"抱住我别松开。我会带你回家的。"

Carol held on to Henry while he pushed his way across the little park in the wind and rain. They went slowly and carefully, looking out for[1] fallen branches and hanging wires. On they went, the whistle of the wind shrill in their ears.

At last they got home and pulled off their wet coats. "That was the worst storm I ever saw," said Carol.

"Carol!" said Henry. "Don't you know? That almost was a hurricane."

He looked worried. The radio was still going because Henry had been in too much of a hurry to turn it off. A voice was saying:

"This is your mayor. I ask you all to stay indoors for several hours. Go out only if you must. Hurricane will bypass Springfield but the wind is very dangerous. There is danger from falling signs and falling wires. Remember, please stay indoors if you can."

"Did you hear that?" Henry asked Carol.

"Yes," said Carol in a small scared voice.

The mayor was still talking when the telephone rang. Henry ran to answer it.

It was his mother.

"Henry," she said, "we're all staying here at work until the wind is a little lower. Are you and Carol all right?"

---

[1] look out for 注意防备

亨利艰难地在风雨中穿过小公园，卡罗尔紧紧地抱住他。他们慢慢地、小心翼翼地走着，防备着断裂的树枝和垂落的电线。他们继续前进，尖利的风声在他们的耳边呼啸着。

最后，他们终于到了家里，脱下湿淋淋的衣服。"这是我所见过的最糟糕的暴风雨，"卡罗尔说。

"卡罗尔！"亨利说，"难道你不知道？那差不多是一场飓风。"

他看起来忧心忡忡。收音机仍在广播着，因为亨利行色匆匆忘了关掉。只听一个声音说道：

"我是你们的市长。请各位都在室内呆几个小时。不到万不得已不要出去。虽然飓风将会绕过斯普林菲尔德市，但仍然非常危险。落下的招牌和电线也非常危险。记住，请尽可能呆在室内。"

"你听见了吗？"亨利问卡罗尔。

"听见了，"卡罗尔恐惧地小声说。

市长仍在讲话，这时电话响了。亨利跑去接。是他的母亲。

"亨利，"他的母亲说，"我们都要呆在单位，等风小点儿再回家。你和卡罗尔没事儿吧？"

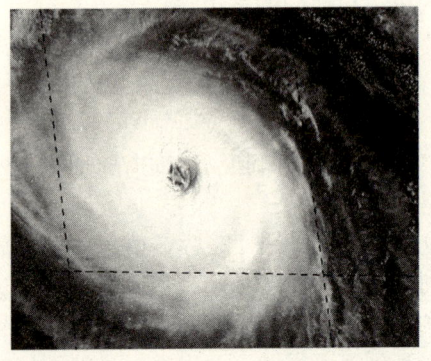

hurricane

"Yes, Mom, we're fine," Henry said. "Carol, come talk to Mom."

Carol took the telephone.

"I'm fine, Mom," she said. "And don't worry. I'll stay indoors. The mayor told me to!"

飓风过后

"没事儿,妈妈,我们都很好,"亨利说,"卡罗尔,来跟妈妈说说话。"

卡罗尔拿起电话。

"我很好,妈妈,"她说,"别担心。我会呆在家里的。是市长教我这样做的!"

The Violets in Spring

In the early morning, in bright spring sunshine, Jennie came back to me. I heard her voice in the hall, and had only time to slip into my coat, before she was up the stairs and in at the door. She had a little suitcase in her hand. She dropped it just inside the doorway, and came flying across the room, and kissed me. The whole sunny, sweet-smelling spring morning had come in with her.

She was dressed in a traveling suit; she even had gloves on. She was breathless, but only from running up the stairs, or from happiness; her brown eyes never faltered[1] as they searched my face. I took a deep breath. "Jennie," I said. "I've missed you."

"I know," she answered. "I've missed you, too. And it's been longer for me." She drew her hands away from mine with sudden gravity[2]. "I'm not in school any more," she said.

"I know," I said. "I can see."

She turned slowly on her heel, and looked around the room. "How I've dreamed of this, Eben," she said. "I can't tell you. The nights I've lain awake, thinking of this room…"

---

[1] falter /ˈfɔːltə/ *vi.* 犹豫
[2] gravity /ˈgrævɪti/ *n.* 引力

春天的紫罗兰

早晨,在明媚的春光中,詹妮回到了我身边。我听到了她在走廊里的声音;在她上楼、进门之前,我只来得及穿上自己的外套。她手里拎着小手提箱,放在门口,就飞奔过来吻我。她带来了春天早晨的明媚阳光和芬芳气息。

她穿着旅行服,甚至还戴着手套。她气喘吁吁,这只是因为她刚跑上楼,或许是出于兴奋;她褐色的眼睛在看我的脸时从来没有迟疑过。我深深地吸了口气,说:"詹妮,我很想你。"

"我知道,"她回答说,"我也想你。而且我想你更多。"她突然将手从我手里抽出来,"我已经不再上学了。"

"我知道,"我说,"我看得出来。"

她慢慢地转动脚跟,环顾了一下房间。"我是多么梦想这个呀,伊本,"她说,"我无法告诉你。我睁眼躺着的那些夜晚,就想到了这个房间……"

She was silent for a moment. "Eben," she said at last. "let's do something special—shall we? To celebrate? Because I haven't really very long to stay with you. You see…I'm being sent abroad—to France—to a finishing school[1] for two years."

She held my hand tight. "I've got to," she said.

For a moment she seemed to be lost in thought[2], her head bent, her eyes hidden under their long lashes[3]. Then she roused[4] herself, and sat up with a smile. "Let's go on a picnic, Eben," she said. "Somewhere in the country—for a whole day—"

"It's something we've never done before." A whole day in the country, in the warm spring weather, together…

She could hardly wait for me to finish my coffee; we hurried down the stairs and out into the street, hand in hand; and the bright sunny morning fell on us like an armful of flowers.

Gus was in his cab, at the corner. When he saw me with Jennie, he took his hat off.

"Where do you want to go, Mack?"

I waved him forward. "Wherever it's green," I said. "Wherever it's country."

---

[1] a finishing school 精修学校（教导女子在上流社会中仪态举止的私立学校，通常学费非常昂贵）
[2] be lost in thought 陷入沉思
[3] lash /læʃ/ *n.* 睫毛
[4] rouse /rauz/ oneself 振作精神；奋起

她沉默了一会儿。"伊本,"她最后说道,"让我们来做一些不同寻常的事情——好吗?庆祝一下?因为我真的有好久没有跟你在一块了。你知道……我要被送到国外去——到法国去——到一所精修学校学习两年。"

她紧紧地握住我的手,说:"我不得不这样。"

一时间,她低着头,似乎陷入了沉思,她的眼睛掩藏在长长的眼睫毛下面。随后,她振作精神,面带微笑坐了起来。"我们去野餐吧,伊本,"她说,"到乡下某个地方——过一整天。"

"这是我们以前从未做过的事情。"在温暖的春天,一块到乡下过上一整天……

她几乎等不及让我喝完咖啡;我们匆匆下楼,手拉手来到了大街上;早晨明媚的阳光犹如一抱鲜花撒落在我们身上。

加斯将出租车停在街角。当看到我和詹妮在一块时,他取下了帽子。

"你们要去哪里,迈克?"

我朝他挥了挥手,说:"只要是有绿色的地方,哪怕是乡下。"

I don't know where we went, but it was green and lovely. It was somewhere north of the city—perhaps in Westchester. It took us about an hour to get there. We left the cab by the roadside, and climbed a fence, and ran across a field with a cow in it. The cow didn't notice us. We climbed a little hill, among some trees. Jennie was flushed and breathless, and full of laughter, she and I ran ahead, and Gus came after us.

At noon we sat together on a warm stonewall in the sun at the edge of a meadow, and near a little wood. There were yellow dandelions in the grass, and the air was sweet as honey. We had some sandwiches along—lettuce[1] and bread for Jennie, sausage[2] for Gus and me. We ate our sandwiches, and drank some beer out of cans. It was the first beer Jennie had ever tasted, she didn't like it, she said it tasted bitter.

Gus and Jennie did most of the talking. Jennie sat on the wall beside me, her head against my shoulder. She had twined[3] a yellow dandelion in her hair, it gave out a fresh, weedy fragrance. The sky was robin[4]'s eggs; I heard a bird singing in the woods. I was happy—happier than I had ever been before, happier than I've ever been since.

---

[1] lettuce /ˈletis/ n. 莴苣
[2] sausage /ˈsɔsidʒ; (US) ˈsɔːsidʒ/ n. 香肠
[3] twine /twain/ vt. 给…戴花冠
[4] robin /ˈrɔbin/ n. 知更鸟

我不知道要去哪里，但那应该是绿色和可爱的地方。是城市北部的某个地方——也许是在温切斯特。我们赶到那里大约需要一个小时。我们将出租车停到路边，爬过一个篱笆，跑过一片田地，田地里有一头奶牛。那头奶牛没有注意到我们。我们爬上了一座掩映在树丛中的小小山丘。詹妮满脸通红，气喘吁吁，而且笑声朗朗。她和我跑在前头，加斯跟在我们后边。

中午时分，我们一块在草地边的一块暖石上坐下来晒太阳。草地靠近一片小树林，草丛中有黄色的蒲公英，空气像蜜一样甜。我们带来了一些三明治——詹妮吃着莴苣和面包，我和加斯吃香肠。我们吃了三明治，然后喝了一些罐装啤酒。这是詹妮第一次品尝啤酒，她不喜欢喝，她说啤酒很苦。

多数时间都是加斯和詹妮在说话。詹妮坐在我身边的墙上，头靠着我的肩膀。她在头发里插了一朵黄色的蒲公英，蒲公英散发出新鲜而清新的芳香。天空像知更鸟蛋一样；我听到小鸟在树林中鸣唱。我感到非常高兴——比以前任何时候都高兴，比有生以来任何时候都高兴。

Gus left us after lunch, and went back to the cab, to take a nap. Then Jennie too grew silent, resting against me, dreamy and content[1]. After a while, I felt her stir, and draw a long, uneven breath. "What are you thinking, Jennie?" I asked.

She answered slowly and gently, "I'm thinking how beautiful the world is, Eben; and how it keeps on being beautiful—no matter what happens to us; the sun goes down in the same green, lovely sky; the birds sing…for us, or for yesterday…or for tomorrow. It was never made for anything but beauty, Eben—whether we lived now, or long ago."

"Tomorrow," I said. "But when is tomorrow, Jennie?"

"Does it matter?" she asked.

"Yes. Promise me you'll never forget."

I sang softly:

"*Where I come from,*
Nobody knows,
And where I'm going,
Everything goes."

She took it up with a little cry of surprise:

"*The wind blows,*
The sea flows—
And God knows."

And she lifted her lips to mine.

---

[1] content /'kɔntent/ *a.* 满足的

午饭后,加斯离开了我们,回到出租车里去午休。随后,詹妮也渐渐不吭声了,靠着我,睡眼朦胧,是那样惬意。过了一会儿,我感到她动了一下,长吁一口气。"你在想什么,詹妮?"我问。

她轻柔地答道:"我在想世界是多么美丽,伊本;怎样一直保持这种美丽——无论我们发生什么事;太阳就这样在绿色的、可爱的天空下降落;小鸟歌唱……为我们,为昨天……为明天。除了美丽,什么也不要创造,伊本——无论我们是生活在现在还是生活在很久以前。"

"明天,"我说,"但明天是什么时候呢,詹妮?"

"那<u>重要</u>吗?"她问。

"是的。答应我你永远不会忘记。"

我轻轻地吟诵道:

"我来自何方,

　无人知晓,

　我要去何方,

　一切随往。"

她带着吃惊小声接续道:

"风吹,

　海荡——

　上帝明了。"

她向我抬起了芳唇。

Later we walked in the faint green of the woods, through the shadow of branches, over the ferns[1] and the moss. We found a little brook, and violets hidden among their leaves. Jennie stopped to pick them. "It's to remember today," she said.

The sun begun to sink in the west; the shadows fell around us. It grew chilly; we turned, and started home.

---

[1] fern /fəːn/ n. 蕨类植物

之后,我们走在泛着淡绿色的树林里,穿过树枝婆娑的阴影,越过蕨类植物和苔藓,发现了一条小溪,还有掩映在枝叶中的紫罗兰。詹妮停下来采撷。"我是不会忘记今天的,"她说。

太阳开始西沉;夜影笼罩在我们四周。天渐渐转凉;我们转过身,启程回了家。

The View from the 28th Floor

Steve Ryan, up there on the twenty-eighth floor of a San Francisco[1] apartment building, squeezed the binoculars[2] closer to his eyes and groaned helplessly. That old station wagon[3], parked with its wheels turned the wrong way, was creeping down to the steeper part of the street every time a car went by.

Home with a cold, Steve had just been looking over the city when he had seen the car drive up and the driver jump out and go into a building. The front wheels had caught Steve's attention because he knew that on a steep hill the wheels should have been turned toward the curb[4].

"Come back!" Steve called to the driver helplessly, and stared again. He was not mistaken. Even as he watched, a huge truck went by, and the car moved a little farther down the hill.

Something had to be done! He was trying to think, to figure out what to do, when he saw something moving in the car and looked closer. He groaned again.

Oh, no! There was a child in the car!

---

[1] San Francisco /sænfræn'siskəu/ n. 旧金山
[2] binoculars /bi'nɔkjuləz/ n. 双筒望远镜
[3] station wagon 旅行车；客货两用车
[4] curb /kəːb/ n. 路边石

28 层楼上的小男孩

斯蒂芬·瑞安站在旧金山一座公寓楼的 28 层上,将双筒望远镜紧紧地贴住眼睛,无奈地咕哝着。那辆停错地方的旧旅行车正从街边陡峭的坡上滑下来,不时有车从街上经过。

由于感冒呆在家里,斯蒂芬一直在眺望着城市,突然他看到那辆汽车开上来,司机从车里跳出来,走进了一座大楼。前车轮引起了斯蒂芬的注意,因为他知道在陡峭的山上车轮应该是朝向人行道的。

"回来!"斯蒂芬对那个司机无奈地喊道,然后又盯着看。他没错。甚至在他看的当儿,一辆大卡车从那辆车旁边飞驰而过,那辆汽车又向小山下移动了一点。

必须得做点儿什么!他正在设法想着该怎么办,这时他看到那辆汽车里有什么东西在动,就看得更仔细了。他又咕哝了一声。

噢,不!车里有个小孩!

Steve wished there had been someone home to help him decide what to do, but his mother was grocery shopping. From a distance he heard the wailing of a siren [1] and got an idea. The police—call the police!

He put the binoculars down, ran over to the telephone, and dialed the operator.

"May I help you?" a pleasant voice said a moment later.

"Yes, please connect me with the police department," Steve said.

The operator hesitated and then said, "Are you sure you're not playing a joke of some kind?"

"Please—hurry!" Steve replied. "Hurry!"

The tone of Steve's voice must have convinced the operator that Steve was serious because she rang the police department. A man's voice came on the line—"San Francisco Police Department, Officer Connor speaking."

Steve blurted out[2] what he had seen while the policeman listened silently. When Steve had finished the policeman said, "Now take it easy and let's go over your story again. You say you can see a car on the top of a hill over there, and it looks as though it has started to slip downhill?"

"Yes, sir, that's right," replied Steve.

"Where is the car located[3]?" the officer asked.

---

[1] siren /ˈsaiərin/ n. 警报；警笛
[2] blurt out 脱口而出
[3] locate /ləuˈkeit/ vt. 找出

史蒂夫真希望家里有人帮他决定该怎么做，但母亲买东西去了。他听到了远处警笛的呼啸声，于是就有了主意。警察——给警察打电话！

他放下望远镜，跑到电话边，拨通了接线员。

"有什么事吗？"过了一会儿，一个悦耳的声音问道。

"是的，请给我接警察局，"史蒂夫说。

接线员犹豫了一下，然后问："你敢肯定不是恶作剧吧？"

"请——快点儿！"史蒂夫说，"快点儿！"

史蒂夫的语调一定使接线员相信他是认真的，因为她接通了警察局的电话。一个男人的声音从电话里传来——"旧金山警察局，我是康纳警官。"

史蒂夫脱口说出了他所看到的东西，警察默默地听着。史蒂夫说完后，警察说道："现在不要慌，让我们再回顾一下你说的事儿。你是说，你可以看到那里的小山顶上有一辆汽车，而且它好像已经开始向山下滑动？"

"是的，先生，是这样，"史蒂夫回答说。

"那辆汽车在什么位置？"警官问道。

"I can't tell," Steve said desperately. "It's either three or four blocks away from my department. There are other buildings in the way, but I can see the top of the hill from here." He gave the officer his own address.

The officer was silent for a moment and then said, "Hang on for just a minute."

It was quiet for a couple of minutes, then the officer came back on again. "Can you take the phone over by the window?" he asked. He was quiet and gentle, and he made Steve feel better.

"Yes, officer," Steve said, moving over. "I'm by the window now."

"Good, now look out and tell me when you see a helicopter," the policeman replied.

Steve looked, and looked again. At first he didn't see anything. And then he saw a huge old whirlybird[1] beating its way toward him. "I see it."

"Keep an eye on[2] it, and when he gets over your building tell the pilot which way to go."

Steve gulped[3]. "How?" he asked.

The officer chuckled, and it calmed Steve some. "I've got you connected to his radio so he can hear you," he said.

"Loud and clear," another voice said.

In a few seconds the big whirlybird was right out front. Steve said, "Over there—over on the hill."

---

[1] whirlybird /'wəːlibəːd/ *n.* （口）直升机
[2] keep an eye on 密切注意
[3] gulp *vi.* 深呼吸；大喘气

"我说不清楚,"史蒂夫不无失望地说,"离我住的公寓有三四个街区。路上还有别的大楼,但我从这里可以看到小山顶。"他把自己的地址告诉了警官。

警官沉默了一会儿,然后说道:"请别挂断,等一会儿。"

静了两三分钟之后,警官又回到了电话边。"你把电话拿到窗边好吗?"他说。他的声音平静而又温和,使史蒂夫感觉好了些。

"好,警官,"史蒂夫走过去说,"我现在到了窗边。"

"好,现在向外看,当你看到直升机时,就告诉我,"警官回答说。

史蒂夫看啊看。开始,他什么也看不到,随后便看到了一架庞大的老式直升机向他这边飞来。"我看见它了。"

"好好看着它。当飞到你的楼顶上空时,告诉飞行员走哪一条路线。"

史蒂夫深吸了口气,问:"怎么说?"

警官轻声笑了一下,这使史蒂夫平静了些。"我已经将你和他的无线电联上了,所以他可以听到你的声音,"他说。

"声音大点,清晰点,"另一个声音说道。

过了几秒钟,大直升机就到了楼前。史蒂夫说:"在那里——就在那边的小山上。"

helicopter

The big machine swung away. "This way?" the pilot asked.

"No—the other way," Steve shouted. "Move in the opposite direction!"

"Roger[1]," the pilot said, as he turned obediently.

"There—the station wagon is right down below," Steve yelled a minute later.

"Got it," the pilot said. And then he gave the policeman the street names. "I can see the car now, and it is slipping!"

---

[1] roger /'rɔdʒə(r)/ *int.* （无线电通讯答语）明白了；已收到

救援直升飞机

　　大飞机转身飞走了。"是这个方向吗？"飞行员问。

　　"不是——是相反的方向，"史蒂夫大声说道，"向反方向移动！"

　　"明白，"飞行员说着，顺从地转了过去。

　　"在那里——那辆旅行车就在下面，"一分钟后，史蒂夫大声喊道。

　　"明白，"飞行员说。随后，他向那名警察报出了街名。"我现在可以看到那辆汽车了，它正在下滑！"

The whirlybird hovered[1]. Steve gripped the binoculars and tried to keep the phone from slipping, but it was hard. He took a deep breath as the station wagon moved a little faster. Then suddenly a police car pulled up beside it, and a policeman jumped out. He leaped inside the station wagon and pulled the emergency brake. The policeman had stopped the car just in time. The trouble was over!

"O.K. We've got everything under control," the pilot said. Then Officer Connor came on again. "Son, you still there?"

"Yes, sir," Steve answered.

"You saved that child's life!" the officer said gently. "You did a fine job and you have every reason to be proud of yourself."

Steve was still a little shaky when his mother returned with the groceries.

"You're feeling a lot better, aren't you?" she said smiling. "Did you find something while I was gone?"

Steve nodded his head. "I sure did, Mom," he said grinning. "I sure did find something to do."

---

[1] hover /ˈhovə(r)/; (US) ˈhʌvər/ vi. 盘旋

直升机盘旋着。史蒂夫紧紧地抓着望远镜，尽量不让话筒滑落，但这很难做到。当那辆旅行车移动稍微加快时，他深吸了口气。紧接着，一辆警车突然停在了那辆旅行车边，一名警察飞身跳出，纵身跃进那辆旅行车，拉动紧急制动闸。警察及时让那辆汽车停了下来。危机终于过去了！

"好了。我们已经控制了一切，"飞行员说。随后，康纳警官的声音又响了起来："孩子，你还在那里吗？"

"在，先生，"史蒂夫回答说。

"是你救了那个孩子的生命！"警官轻声说道，"你做得很好，你完全有理由为自己感到骄傲。"

母亲买东西回来时，史蒂夫还有点儿颤抖。

"你感觉好多了，不是吗？"她微笑着说，"我不在家时，你发现了什么事儿吗？"

史蒂夫点点头。"我的确发现了，妈妈，"他咧嘴笑道，"我的确发现了值得做的事儿。"

The Pelicans above the Aegean Sea

On a September day in 1985, great flocks of pelicans[1] flew high above the Aegean Sea. They were migrating to African, as they have done through the ages. About 100 miles east of Athens, one young bird—weak, tired and lamed—gave up and fell behind. Far below him lay an island. He glided down to it and settled on a rocky point to rest, perhaps to die.

No one could have foretold what this single weary bird was to mean to the little island of Mykonos. "Nothing had happened here for 5 000 years," says one Mykonian. "And then our pelican came."

The exhausted bird, too crippled to fish for itself, might well have died. But a fisherman happened along in his boat and carried it into port. There it aroused much curiosity and sympathy. Everybody agreed on what to do: "Give it to Theodoros."

Theodoros, a rugged boatman with a huge mustache, is a lover of wildlife. At the time, his tow-room house sheltered several birds and even a baby seal that he was nursing back to health. Theodoros was glad to add the pelican to his charges. He named him Peter.

---

[1] pelican /ˈpelikən/ n. 鹈鹕

爱琴海上的鹈鹕鸟

1985年9月的一天,大群大群的鹈鹕在爱琴海高空飞翔。就像世世代代所做的那样,它们正在向非洲迁徙。在雅典东部大约100英里处,一只小鸟疲惫虚弱、又瘸又拐——落在后面,不想再飞了。在它下面很远处有一座岛。它向下滑翔到这个岛上,栖息在一个岩石嶙峋的岬角,也许是等死。

没人能预言这只疲惫不堪的孤鸟对小小的米克诺斯岛意味着什么。"这里五千年来什么也没发生过,"一位米克诺斯人说,"后来我们的鹈鹕飞来了。"

这只筋疲力尽的鸟伤得太厉害,无法自己抓鱼吃,本来很可能会死去。但一位渔夫碰巧驾船从那里经过,便把它带回了港口。它在港口引起了人们极大的好奇和同情。大家一致同意这样做:"把它送给西奥多罗斯。"

西奥多罗斯是一位倔强的船夫,留着大胡子,非常喜欢野生动物。当时,他的两居室里养着好几只鸟,甚至还有一只小海豹。他正在护理它们使它们恢复健康。西奥多罗斯乐于在监护对象中增加这只鹈鹕。他给这只鹈鹕取名叫彼得。

Peter, petted and spoiled by Theodoros, and fattened by everybody, grew strong and healthy. Soon the Mykonians began to consider him a sort of mascot[1]. Maybe, it was said jokingly, he had been sent by the gods from the sacred island of Delos, nearby. Now, with Peter's help, Mykonos might prosper at last. Fishermen began to wonder if their catches hadn't been bigger lately…

One spring in the migration season, Peter vanished. Anxious inquires went out to the other islands. Soon the Mykonians got an answer which at first cheered them: Peter was safe and sound on the nearby island of Tenos. Then they turned purple with anger. For Tenos refused to give him back.

The Mykonoians appealed to the official in charge of both Mykonos and Tenos. His Excellency[2] listened to arguments from both sides.

The men of Tenos insisted, "This is no tame bird; it is a wild migrant, free to go where it likes. It decided it did not like Mykonos—for reasons we are too polite to suggest—and has of its own will come to us."

The men of Mykonos retorted, "What nonsense! We saved Peter, fed him, cared for him as for our children. He is young bird, easily confused. It was only bad navigation or, more likely, a strong wind that carried him to Tenos against his will. He is ours!"

---

[1] mascot /'mæskət/ *n.* 吉祥鸟
[2] His Excellency /'eksələnsi/ 阁下

彼得受到西奥多罗斯的宠爱和娇惯，大家又把它喂得肥肥的，所以它长得既结实又健康。不久，米克诺斯人开始把它看作是一种吉祥物。人们开玩笑说，也许它是众神从附近神圣的得洛斯岛派来的。现在，在彼得的帮助下，米克诺斯终于得以繁荣。渔民们也开始希望他们最近捕的鱼能多一些……

在迁徙季节的一个春天，彼得突然不见了。人们焦虑地向别的岛屿打听消息。不久，米克诺斯人得到了答复：彼得在附近的蒂诺斯岛，安然无恙。起初，他们一听很高兴。但接着他们气得脸都发紫了，因为蒂诺斯人拒绝归还彼得！

米克诺斯人向兼管米克诺斯岛和蒂诺斯岛的官员上诉。这位官员阁下听取了双方的论点。

蒂诺斯人坚持认为："这并不是一只驯养鸟；它是一只野生候鸟，它爱去哪里就去哪里。这只鸟认定它不喜欢米克诺斯——出于礼貌，我们不便说出原因。它来我们这里是它自己的意愿。"

米克诺斯人则反驳说："胡说八道！是我们救了彼得，喂它食物，像照顾我们的孩子那样照顾它。它是一只小鸟，容易犯糊涂。它去蒂诺斯只能是飞行失误，要么多半是一股强风把它吹到了蒂诺斯，这是违背它本意的。它是我们的。"

At last, the official announced his decision, "The bird belongs to Mykonos. Tell the police in Tenos to let them have him."

Peter returned home in glory. Everybody on Mykonos dropped work and crowded around the harbor. Church bells rang joyously. The minute the gangplank[1] was down, Peter pushed ahead to walk down it first. He seemed aware of his own importance.

The Mykonians took no more risks. Around one of Peter's legs they put a silver nameplate reading Mykonos. To make sure he would never fly away again, Theodoros took out a few feathers from one wing, explaining, "He is not hurt; he can fly a little for exercise, but not far."

At first, Peter was famous only in Greece. Later, his fame spread around the world. Here is how it happened.

On a warm July evening in 1991, Theodoros was talking about his favorite bird. "Peter is not happy!" he said. "He goes off by himself; he stands on the shore alone, staring out to sea. What is wrong with him? He needs a mate!"

By great luck one of his listeners was from Louisiana, which proudly calls itself the Pelican State. This man got in touch with Louisiana's governor, who sent out an order to his wildlife people: "Find a mate for this Greek pelican."

---

[1] gangplank /ˈgæŋplæŋk/ n. 步桥

最后，那位官员作了裁决："这只鸟属于米克诺斯岛。"然后吩咐蒂诺斯警察让他们把鸟带走。

彼得荣归故里。米克诺斯差不多人人都放下工作，拥到港口周围。教堂响起了欢快的钟声。跳板刚放下，彼得就冲上前第一个走下跳板。它似乎意识到了自己的重要性。

米克诺斯人未敢再冒风险。他们在彼得的一条腿上套上了银质的姓名牌，上面有"米克诺斯"字样。为了确保它永远不再飞走，西奥多罗斯从它的一个翅膀上取下了一些羽毛。他解释说："它没伤着，可以飞上一小段距离活动活动，但飞不远。"

最初，彼得只在希腊有名气。后来，它的名气传遍了世界。事情是这样的：

1991年7月的一个炎热的夜晚，西奥多罗斯正在谈他心爱的鸟儿。"彼得不快活！"他说，"它常常独自走开，独自站在岸边凝望大海。它怎么了？它需要伴侣！"

真是幸运极了，听他讲这番话的听众中有一位来自美国路易斯安那州，路易斯安那州自豪地称自己为鹈鹕州。这个人与路易斯安那州的州长取得了联系。州长向负责野生动物的人下了一道命令："为这只希腊鹈鹕寻找一位伴侣。"

Alphonse

Game wardens[1] combed the swamps and came up with two white pelicans, which they named "Alphonse" and "Omega." The birds made the 6500-mile trip by air, in fancy cages, proudly marked "Playmates for Peter."

When they arrived in Mykonos on December 2, 1991, the island celebrated all day long.

At the welcoming party Peter appeared decked[2] out in a red bow tie. The acting mayor read telegram from Greek admirers wishing the birds long life.

For Alphonse, unfortunately, this was not to be. He had become ill during the long journey, and soon died. When Omega looked bad, too, she was rushed to a veterinarian on a neighboring island. Weeks later, her health restored, she was returned to Mykonos—only to find a rival.

A French film company, come to make a film about Mykonos and Peter, had brought their own mate for him. She is named Irene.

---

[1] game warden （一个地区的）渔猎法执法官
[2] deck　*vt.* 装饰；打扮（out）

阿方斯和奥美加

渔猎执法官们在沼泽地里到处搜寻,找到了两只白鹈鹕。他们给一只取名叫阿方斯,给另一只取名叫奥美加。这两只鸟被装在特制的笼子里,乘飞机旅行了 6500 英里。笼子上自豪地写着"彼得的伴侣"。

1991 年 12 月 2 日,它们到达米克诺斯时,岛上的人庆祝了一整天。

彼得打着红色蝴蝶结参加了欢迎宴会。代理市长宣读了希腊景慕者们打来的祝福这些鸟长寿的电报。

不幸的是,阿方斯没能长寿。它在漫长的旅途中染病,很快就死了。当奥美加也身体欠佳时,人们赶紧把它送向邻近岛上的一位兽医那里。几周后,它终于痊愈,被送回了米克诺斯——结果却发现一个对手正在等着它。

法国的一家电影公司来拍一部关于米克诺斯和彼得的电影,也为彼得带来了一个伴侣,取名叫艾琳。

Theodoros says Peter is much more cheerful now that he has companions. Though he seemed a little jealous of them at first, he has found that they

are no competition. On the island, Peter is the pelican. He has personality; he paddles in the harbor, snoozes on the sandy beach, struts¹ around as boss. He is a clown and a ham. When anybody lifts a camera within a hundred yards of him, he freezes in a dignified pose.

In the old days Peter sometimes wandered around the café begging food, or into butcher shops or even into private homes. Once he lifted a latch with his beak. Householders were honored by such visits, considering them to be good omens.

When thirsty, Peter tries to open a water spigot² on the dock. He has never succeeded, but he doesn't need to: anybody who sees him tugging vainly at the spigot rushes over and draws him enough to drink.

In his clumsy, friendly way, Peter sometimes plays "football" with Theodoros, batting a small balloon around. If anybody pretends to attack Theodoros, Peter dashes up with ruffled feathers and jabbing beak to defend him.

---

[1] strut /strʌt/ *vi.* 趾高气扬地走，高视阔步
[2] spigot /ˈspigət/ *n.* 龙头

西奥多罗斯说,彼得现在有了同伴,快乐多了。虽然彼得开始时有点儿嫉妒两个同伴,但发现它们不是它的对手。在米克诺斯岛上,人们提起鹈鹕时,那指的只是彼得。它总是与众不同;它在港口嬉水,在沙滩上小憩,像老板似的昂首阔步地走来走去。它是一个小丑,也是一个表演过火的演员。要是有人在离它100码处举起相机,它便摆出一副惟我独尊的架势让人拍。

过去,彼得有时在咖啡店游来荡去,求人家喂它食吃,要么就到肉店,甚至到私人家里去。有一次,它用嘴掀开了人家的门闩。房主对这种拜访会感到荣幸,把这看作是好兆头。

彼得渴时,便试着打开码头上的水龙头。它从未成功过,但也无须成功:人们一看到它用力拽水龙头而又拽不开时,便急忙上前放出足够的水给它喝。

彼得有时以笨拙而友好的方式同西奥多罗斯玩足球,把一只小气球击来击去。要是有人假装向西奥多罗斯发动攻击,彼得便急忙冲上前用嘴啄着去保护他。

Toursits often buy fish for the pelicans. When Peter was alone, fishermen used to throw part of their catch to him. But pelicans are greedy. If they were allowed to, each of Mykonos's three birds would gulp down 20 pounds of fish a day. "So," explains the mayor. "We may be the only town in the world—anyway, in Greece—with a fund for the feeding of pelicans."

No taxpayer has complained. On the contrary, as one shopkeeper told me, "It's only right that Mykonos should feed Peter, because Peter helps feed Mykonos." And he does! For a good part of the island's tourist boom can be credited to Peter.

Ten years before he came, Mykonos was known only to a handful of tourists, who liked its quiet, friendly charm and low prices. They liked its ancient windmills, some of them still turning to grind out wheat for the islanders' bread. They liked the simple cube-like houses, all dazzling white. Most of the homes are whitewashed afresh every week.

Now everybody seems to know about Mykonos. I have seen a folder advertising Aegean cruises which ranks Peter almost on a par with Greece's famous art treasures. In Mykonian shops you can find his picture on dishes and seashells, or woven large into the Mykonians' popular woolen bags.

游客们经常买鱼喂这几只鹈鹕。当彼得独自呆着时，渔民们常常把捕到的鱼扔一些给它吃。但鹈鹕们非常贪婪。如果允许它们放开肚子，米克诺斯的三只鸟每只每天要吃掉 20 磅鱼。"所以，"市长解释说，"我们可能是世界上——至少也是全希腊——惟一设有喂养鹈鹕基金的城市。"

纳税人毫无怨言。相反，正如一名店主给我说的那样："米克诺斯喂养彼得是应该的，因为彼得也养活了米克诺斯。"确实如此！米克诺斯岛旅游业兴旺发达，很大程度上应当归功于彼得。

在彼得到来以前的 10 年，知道米克诺斯的游客寥寥无几。他们喜欢这个岛宁静友好、富有魅力，而且价廉物美；他们喜欢岛上古老的风车，其中有些风车迄今仍在转动，为岛民们磨麦粉做面包；他们喜欢那些朴素的立方体状的房子，那些房子白得使人眼花。大多数家庭每周都要重新粉刷一次。

如今，人们都知道米克诺斯了。我看到过一种为促使人们乘船去爱琴海旅游作宣传的小册子，那上面把彼得和希腊著名的艺术珍宝几乎相提并论。在米克诺斯的商店里，你会在盘子上和海贝上看到它的照片，或者看到它的大幅肖像被织在米克诺斯人喜爱的毛织提袋上。

Peter

Visitors sometimes wonder what Mykonians would do if Peter died. Here the scientists have a word of cheer. His species can expect a lifetime of 40 years or more. So Peter should be ruling his grateful kingdom for a good many years to come.

彼 得

　　游客们有时会问：要是彼得死了，米克诺斯人可怎么办？科学家们对此有令人兴奋的说法。彼得这种鸟的寿命可望达到 40 年甚至更长，因此彼得在对它感恩戴德的王国还可以统治好多年。

The Sea Watcher

Thorfinn watched the eagle soar[1] higher and higher. Then, as swift as an arrow, it fell, catching its prey[2] in the mid-flight.

"Over there," Thorfinn said, pointing. "High above the Sea Watcher's Rock."

"I can barely see the Rock, much less an eagle above it," complained Eric. "Thorfinn, your eyes are better than the eagle's. You can see farther than anyone in the village."

Thorfinn turned and looked at his older brother. "Then why won't they let watch for Father's ship?" he asked.

"You know why," Eric replied. "Only the captain's eldest son can be the Sea Watcher."

"Even though he can't see well enough to find the eagle," Thorfinn said in disgust[3].

Eric sighed. "Come on," he said. "I'll race you home. Last one there must clean all the fish."

The brothers raced along the beach to the Viking village, sand flying beneath their bare feet. They arrived, breathless and laughing, at their stone hut. Thorfinn won the race by a yard.

---

[1] soar /sɔː(r)/ *vi.* 翱翔
[2] prey /preɪ/ *n.* 猎物
[3] in disgust /dɪsˈɡʌst/ 讨厌地

望海少年

索芬望着鹰越飞越高。随后，鹰在飞行中像箭一样飞快地扑向猎物。

"在那里，"索芬用手指着说，"在望海岩上空。"

"我几乎看不到望海岩，更不要说上面的鹰了，"埃里克抱怨说，"索芬，你的眼睛比鹰眼还要尖。你比村里任何人看得都远。"

索芬转过头看着哥哥。"那他们为什么不让我守望父亲的轮船呢？"他问。

"你知道为什么，"埃里克回答说，"只有船长的大儿子才能成为望海人。"

"即便他看得不够远找不到鹰，"索芬厌恶地说。

埃里克叹了口气，说："得了吧，我跟你赛跑回家。谁落后谁洗鱼。"

兄弟俩沿着沙滩飞快地向维京村跑去，沙子在他们脚下飞起。他们笑着跑到他们家的小石屋，上气不接下气。索芬比哥哥快了一码，赢得了这场比赛。

He lifted the rough hide that covered the hut's entrance. His mother was rolling dough[1], her strong hands kneading[2] it smooth. Grandfather sat by the fire. His hands were as knotted as the fishnet he was mending.

"I see your luck continues," Mother said as the brother held up their dripping fish. "Whose turn is it to clean them?"

Thorfinn smiled and handed his fish to Eric, who went outside to scrape[3] them. Thorfinn drew close to the fire. Several times he almost turned to Grandfather with the question that burned as hot inside him as the dancing flames.

"The fisherman looks sad," said Grandfather. "Maybe he took many fish from their homes?"

"No, Grandfather. Fishing doesn't make me sad." Then his thoughts slipped out. "Why must the eldest son be the only one allowed to watch for Father's ship? Why not the one with best eyes?"

Grandfather sighed. "Why, you ask. Why, I cannot tell you. It has always been done that way. It will always be, until someone proves that a new way is better."

---

[1] dough /dəu/   *n.* 面团
[2] knead /ni:d/   *vt.* 拧
[3] scrape /skreip/   *vt.* 刮除

他拿起盖在小屋入口的粗糙兽皮。他妈妈在擀面皮,她有劲的双手将面擀得光溜溜的。爷爷坐在火边,两只手像他正在补的鱼网那样疙疙瘩瘩。

"我知道你会好运不断的,"当弟弟举起水淋淋的鱼时,他妈妈说,"这次轮到谁洗它们了?"

索芬微微一笑,将鱼递给了埃里克。埃里克走到外面去剥皮。索芬靠近火边。他好几次都快要转向爷爷问那个问题,那个问题像跳动的火焰一样在他的体内熊熊燃烧着。

"那个渔夫看上去很伤心,"他爷爷说,"也许他从家里拿了好多鱼吧。"

"不是,爷爷。捕鱼没有使我伤心,"随后,他的想法就滑了出来。"为什么只有大儿子才能守望爸爸的船?为什么不允许眼睛最好的儿子守望呢?"

他爷爷叹了口气。"你问的问题,我也说不清。一向都是那样做的,还会永远继续下去,直到有人证明有一种更好的新方法。"

That night Thorfinn lay awake. The ship and its crew had been gone a month longer than his father had said they would be. This was the stormy season, and already several had storms had come. Thorfinn wished his father were home safely, sleeping in the hut with the family.

Thorfinn tossed and turned under the warm sealskin. The night was still. No wind blew in from the ocean. He heard the shepherd's dog bark on a far away hillside. Then, like a fresh breeze filling a limp sail, came an idea.

Thorfinn got up with the sun. He put a long loaf of fresh bread into his bag and crept silently to Grandfather's bedside. The older man was awake.

"I'm going to the hill to help Johan with the sheep," Thorfinn whispered. "Please tell Mother I will return in a few days."

Grandfather nodded his white head. His smile told Thorfinn that he understood the plan.

Far away on the hill Thorfinn saw small white dots he knew to be Johan's sheep. As he drew closer, he called, "Johan! May I visit you for a few days?"

"You are most welcome at my rocky home," Johan replied.

那天夜里,索芬躺在那里睡不着。轮船和船员已经走一个月了,这要比他爸爸所说的时间长。这是暴风季节,而且已经来了好几场猛烈的暴风雨。索芬希望爸爸能平安到家,同家人睡在小屋子里。

索芬在温暖的海豹皮下辗转反侧。夜静静的。没有风从海洋上吹进来。他听到牧羊犬在远处山上的吠叫声。随后,像一阵新鲜的微风鼓满扁扁的船帆一样,他想到了一个主意。

太阳出来了,索芬从床上起来,将一块长面包放进包里,悄悄地爬到爷爷的床边。老人醒了。

"我要去山上帮约翰看羊,"索芬低声说,"请告诉妈妈我过几天就回来了。"

爷爷点了点白发苍苍的头。爷爷的微笑表明他知道这个计划。

索芬看到了远处山上小小的白点,知道那是约翰的羊。当他走近时,他大声喊道:"约翰!我可以帮你看几天吗?"

"你在我的山上是最受欢迎的,"约翰答道。

Inside the small shelter, the boys sat by a blazing[1] fire, talking about the village and eating dried fish and Thorfinn's bread. Through the shepherd's open door, Thorfinn saw the wide ocean stretching westward to the edge of the world. Somewhere out there was his father. Somewhere nearby, Thorfinn hoped.

All day the boys herded[2] the hungry sheep to fresh grass. The eastern ocean was hidden by the steep ridge[3] behind them. But Thorfinn's eyes often slipped to the western horizon, to search for the sail of a returning ship.

That night several climbed to the top of the ridge. The sea unfolded around the entire island in every direction. Searching the western waters, his sharp eyes found no sail. Then, turning eastward to look for the lost sheep, he caught the glimmer of something moving upon the water.

A ship? he thought hopefully. No. Father will be coming from the west, not the east.

Thorfinn squinted against the sun until his eyes ached. Then once more he saw it—a ship, but one with no sail. It was disabled, rocking[4] sideways upon the ocean swells[5].

---

[1] blazing /'bleiziŋ/ *a.* 炽燃的
[2] herd /həːd/ *vt.* 放牧
[3] ridge /ridʒ/ *n.* 山岭
[4] rock *vt.* 摇晃
[5] swell /swel/ *n.* 海面的缓慢起伏（有浪而无浪花）

走进小棚子,两个男孩坐在熊熊燃烧的火边,一边谈论着村子里的事儿,一边吃着干鱼和索芬的面包。通过牧羊人敞开的门,索芬看到宽阔的海洋向西延伸到了世界边缘。父亲就在那里的某个地方。索芬希望就在附近某个地方。

整整一天,两个男孩将饥饿的羊赶到了新鲜的草地。东边的海洋被他们后面陡峭的山岭遮住了。但索芬的眼睛经常溜到西边的地平线上,搜寻着归航的船帆。

那天夜里,他好几次爬到山岭顶上。大海在整个岛四周向各个方向展开。他犀利的眼睛搜寻着西边水域,没有发现船帆。随后,转向东边寻找失踪的羊,他隐隐约约可以看见有什么东西在水面移动着。

轮船?他满怀希望地想道,不,爸爸是从西边而不是东边回来的。

索芬眯眼看着太阳,直到眼睛刺疼。随后,他又一次看到了那个东西——是一艘轮船,但是一艘没有帆的船。那艘船已经失灵,在海浪中歪歪斜斜地摇晃着。

Forgetting the sheep, Thorfinn dashed down the hill, flashing past an astonished Johan. He raced into the village. "A ship!" he cried. "I saw a ship on the eastern waters!"

Women and children poured from their huts. Fishermen on shore pushed Thorfinn into a fishing boat, and he pointed the way to the disabled ship. As they approached, Thorfinn could see the weary faces of the crew. His father gripped the tiller[1] weakly.

The fishing boat pulled alongside the ship. Thorfinn threw a long rope to his father, and the damaged craft[2] was towed safely into harbor.

Later, after a rest, Thorfinn's father gathered the villagers together to tell of the voyage.

"Gusting[3] winds forced us off course and shredded[4] our sails, snapping the mast[5] off as it were rotten wood," he said. "We sailed completely past the island. For days we rowed back, our food and water gone. Then yesterday we spotted the island, but we were too weak to row. If it hadn't been for Thorfinn's sharp eyes, no one would have spotted us until it was too late."

He gave Thorfinn a tired smile. Then he continued in a stronger voice.

---

[1] tiller /ˈtilə/ n. 舵柄
[2] craft /krɑːft/ n. 小船、轮船或飞机
[3] gusting a. 起大风的；多阵风的
[4] shred /ʃred/ vt. 撕裂
[5] mast /mɑːst; (US) mæst/ n. 桅杆

索芬忘记了那些羊,从山上冲下来,从满脸惊讶的约翰身边飞奔而过,跑进了村里。"轮船!"他大声叫道,"我在东边水面上看见一艘船!"

女人们和孩子们从小屋子里涌了出来。岸上的渔夫将索芬推进了一艘渔船。随后,他指了指那艘失灵的船。当他们靠近时,索芬可以看到船员们疲惫不堪的脸。索芬的父亲有气无力地抓着船舵。

小渔船靠近那艘轮船。索芬将一条长绳扔给他父亲。之后,那艘受到损坏的轮船被安全地拖进了港口。

之后,休息了一会儿,索芬的父亲将村里人叫到一块,讲述了这次航行。

"狂风迫使我们偏离了航道,刮坏了船帆,折断了桅杆,好像那是朽木一般,"他说,"我们完全驶离了这座岛。我们往回划了好几天,吃的喝的都没了。昨天,我们看到了这座岛,但我们已经划不动了。要不是索芬眼尖,谁也不会注意到我们,到那时候可就晚了。"

他疲惫地朝索芬笑了笑。随后,他提高嗓门说道:

"For as long as the village can remember, the Sea Watcher has been the captain's eldest son. Our ship's misfortune has shown the folly of such a tradition. Let it be decided that the Sea Watcher will be the one with the best eyes. Our new Sea Watcher is Thorfinn."

"村里人都记得,望海人一直是船长的大儿子。我们的船遭遇的不幸已经表明,这种传统的做法非常愚蠢。由此,我们决定,望海人将是眼睛最好的儿子。我们新的望海人是索芬。"

The Rainbow

Once upon a time the colors of the world started to quarrel. All claimed[1] that they were the best, the most important, the most useful, the most beautiful, the favorite.

Green said, "Clearly I'm the most important. I'm the symbol of life and of hope. I was chosen for grass, trees and leaves. Without me, all animals will die. Look over the countryside and you will see that I'm in the majority."

Blue cut short[2], "You only think about the land, but consider the sky and the sea. It's the water that is the basis of life and drawn up by the clouds from the deep sea. The sky gives space, peace and serenity[3]. Without my peace, you would all be nothing."

Yellow chuckled[4], "You're all so serious. I bring laughter, happiness, and warmth into the world. The sun is yellow, the moon is yellow and the stars are yellow. Every time you look at a sunflower, the whole world starts to smile. Without me there would be no fun."

---

[1] claim *vt.* 声称；主张
[2] cut short 打断
[3] serenity /si'reniti/ *n.* 平静
[4] chuckle *vi.* 吃吃地笑

彩虹一家亲

从前,世界上的色彩发生了争吵。它们都声称自己是最优秀、最重要、最有用、最漂亮、最可人的色彩。

绿色说:"显然,我是最重要的色彩。我是生命和希望的象征。我被选为了青草、树木和叶子的色彩。没有我,所有动物都会死去。眺望乡野,你就会看到满眼都是我的色彩。"

蓝色打断说:"你只想到了陆地上的色彩,但想想天空和海洋。水是生命的基础,由云彩从深海里吸上来。天空赋予空间、和平与宁静。没有我的和平,你们将什么也不是。"

黄色轻声笑道:"你们都这样一本正经。我给这个世界带来了笑声、欢乐和温暖。太阳是黄色的,月亮是黄色的,星星也是黄色的。每次你们看向日葵,全世界都开始微笑。没有我,就不会有什么乐趣。"

Orange started next to blow her trumpet, "I'm the color of health and strength. I may be scarce, but I'm precious, for I serve the needs of human life. I carry the most important vitamins. Think of carrots[1], pumpkins, oranges, mangoes and papayas[2]. I don't hang around all the time, but when I fill the sky at sunrise or sunset, my beauty is so striking[3] that no one gives another thought to any of you."

Red could stand it on longer. He shouted, "I'm the ruler of all of you. I'm blood—life's blood! I'm the color of danger and of bravery. I'm willing to fight for a cause. I bring fire into the blood. Without me the earth would be an empty as the moon. I'm the color of passion and of love, the red rose, the poinsettia[4] and the poppy[5]."

Purple rose up to his full height. He was very tall and spoke with great pomp[6], "I'm the color of royalty and power. Kings, chiefs and bishops have always chosen me, for I'm the symbol of authority[7] and wisdom. People do not question me! They listen and obey."

---

[1] carrot *n.* 胡萝卜
[2] papaya /pə'paiə/ *n.* 番木瓜果（树）
[3] striking *a.* 显著的；惊人的
[4] poinsettia /pɔin'setiə/ *n.* 猩猩木
[5] poppy *n.* 罂粟
[6] pomp *n.* 夸耀；壮丽
[7] authority /ɔː'θɔriti/ *n.* 权威

紧接着，橙色开始自吹自擂："我是健康和力量的色彩。我可能不多见，但很珍贵，因为我能迎合人类生活的需要。我含有最重要的维生素。想想胡萝卜、南瓜、橘子、芒果和木瓜。

尽管我不是一直露面，但当日出或日落我弥漫天空时，我的美丽是那样引人注目，谁也不会去想你们。"

红色再也忍不住了，它大声嚷道："我是你们所有色彩的统治者。我是血——生命之血！我是危险和勇敢的色彩。我愿意为事业而奋斗。我把火融进血液。没有我，地球将像月球一样空空荡荡。我是情与爱的色彩，是红玫瑰、猩猩木与罂粟的色彩。"

紫色站直了身体，它个子高大，不可一世地说："我是王位和权力的色彩。国王、首领和主教总是选我，因为我是权威和智慧的象征。人们不会质疑我。他们惟命是从。"

Finally Indigo spoke quietly, "Think of me. I'm the color of silence. You hardly notice me, but without me you all become shallow. I represent thought and reflection, twilight and deep water. You need me for balance and contrast, for prayer and inner peace."

So the colors went on boasting[1], their quarrel getting louder and louder. Suddenly there was a startling flash of bright lightning, thunder rolled and boomed. Rain started to pour down. The colors crouched down[2] in fear, drawing close to one another for comfort.

In the midst of the clamor, the rain began to speak, "You silly colors, fighting amongst yourselves, each trying to dominate[3] the rest. Don't you know that you were each made for a special purpose, unique and different? Join hands with one another and come to me."

Doing as they were told, the colors united and joined hands.

The rain continued, "From now on, when it rains, each of you will stretch across the sky in a great bow of color as a reminder that you can all live in peace. The rainbow is a symbol of hope for tomorrow."

And so, whenever a good rain rinses[4] the world, and a rainbow appears in the sky.

---

[1] boast *vi.* 自夸
[2] crouch down 蹲下来
[3] dominate /'dɒmineit/ *vt.* 支配；占优势
[4] rinse /rins/ *vt.* 冲洗；清洗

最后，青色平静地说："想想我吧。我是寂静的色彩。你们几乎注意不到我，但没有我，你们将会变得浅薄。我代表思想与反思、微光与深水。你们需要我来平衡和对比，需要我去祈祷与静心。"

色彩们继续自吹自擂，争吵声越来越大。突然，电闪雷鸣，大雨倾盆。色彩们恐惧地蹲下身子，相互靠近，以求安慰。

在喧闹声中，雨开口说道："你们这些傻色彩，发生内讧，每个人都想支配别人。难道你们不知道每种色彩都是为一种特殊的目的——独一无二、与众不同的目的而造出来的吗？手拉手到我这里来！"

色彩们按照雨说的手拉手，团结在了一起。

雨接着说道："从现在起，每当下雨时，你们每一种色彩都要横跨天空，形成一道巨大的彩虹，提醒你们能够和平相处。彩虹是明天希望的象征。"

于是，无论什么时候一场好雨清洗这个世界，一道彩虹就会出现在天空中。

The Koalas' New Home

A koala mother with her baby riding "piggy back" slows drivers down to a turtle's pace as she crosses a busy road. Mindless of any danger, she ambles[1] in an awkward motion with but one thing in mind: She must find a good eating tree—a new home for herself and her baby.

The tired mother keeps going, a break in the busy day for drivers who wait patiently for the koalas to cross the road. Australians put the "koala crossing" signs and know the importance of saving their valuable animals.

The January day is hot and a smell of smoke hangs heavy in the air. It comes from the burning forest which the koalas were forced to leave. Now homeless, they cannot know the problems awaiting them in the outside world, nor do they realize their good fortune in escaping at all. Many have perished[2].

Sometimes, when the burden is too great, the mother shakes her little one down from her back. She is ten months old now and must learn to walk more by herself.

---

[1] amble /ˈæmbl/   vi. 缓行；轻跑
[2] perish /ˈperiʃ/   vi. 丧生

考拉熊的新家

考拉熊妈妈带着它那驮在背上的孩子穿过繁华的马路,使司机的速度慢得像海龟爬行一样。它不管有什么危险,一直以笨拙的动作缓步而行,脑子里只想着一件事:它必须找到一棵好吃的树——为自己和孩子找一个新家。

这个疲倦的母亲不停地走着,造成繁忙的车流在大白天陷于停顿,司机们都耐心地等待考拉熊走过马路。澳大利亚人挂出了"考拉熊横穿马路"的告示,他们知道保护这些珍稀动物的重要性。

一月的天气很热,空气中弥漫着浓烟的味道。烟是从燃烧的森林里飘出的,这使考拉熊被迫离开了那里。现在,它们无家可归,还不知道外面的世界有多少问题在等着它们,也没意识到它们能逃生是多么幸运。好多考拉熊都已经死了。

有时,考拉熊妈妈觉着负担太重,就把小熊从背上放下来。它已经10个月大了,必须自己学着多走走路。

Later, the koalas stop to rest under a tree and the mother tests it by pressing her black leathery nose against the trunk. Her nose tells her it is not good for eating, but will do to rest in. Then the leaves move, as they climb hand over hand high into the tree's branches where they sit huddled[1] for a short time. Then the mother allows her baby to crawl into her bag and they both fall asleep.

Darkness comes and hunger comes to the orphans from the bush to continue on. Two days have passed without a good feeding of leaves. But the mother is choosy. There are many kinds of leaves but so few that she likes.

So far, the little fire victims have been lucky. They have not been injured or killed by a car or attacked by a dog. News reporters keep the public well informed and citizens are watchful. They even try to keep their dogs from running after the koalas.

At dawn, the mother koala finally locates[2] a good eating tree but is unaware that it belongs to humans. Good, she pulls greedily on the lush[3] green leaves, then chews some for her little one who cannot, as yet, eat them whole. Then, happy and content, the tired travelers fall asleep.

---

[1] huddle /'hʌdl/ vi. 群集；聚在一起
[2] locate /ləu'keit/ vt. 找到；查明
[3] lush /lʌʃ/ a. 青葱的；草木茂盛的；多汁的；味美的；芬芳的

后来，考拉熊母子俩在一棵树下停下来休息。熊妈妈把它黑黝黝、毛茸茸的鼻子贴在这棵树上嗅擦。它的鼻子告诉它这棵树的叶子不好吃，但可以在树上休息做窝。当它们双手交替往树上爬时，树叶摇曳，它们在树枝上蹲伏一会儿。随后，熊妈妈让孩子躺在它的育儿袋里，双双便倒头睡去。

黑暗降临。树枝上的孤儿寡母仍在挨饿。两天过去了，它们没好好吃过一顿树叶。熊妈妈非常挑剔，虽然有很多种树叶，但它喜欢的却寥寥无几。

直到现在，这两个火灾的小小受害者都很幸运。它们既没有受伤，也没有被汽车撞死或被狗咬。新闻报道向大众随时报道此事，同时市民们也在密切关注着，甚至设法不让自家的狗去追那些考拉熊。

到黎明时分，考拉熊妈妈终于找到了一棵好吃的树，但它没有意识到，这是属于人类的。太好吃了，它贪婪地爬上树，摘下鲜嫩多汁的绿叶，为它的小宝宝嚼碎一些树叶，因为小考拉熊还不能吃整片的树叶。随后，又困又乏的母子俩心满意足地进入了梦乡。

Awakening later, the mother shakes herself from head to foot, drawing her back claws through her thick brown coat. Next comes baby, who gets a thorough bath with her tongue. When done, the mother koala stops to look sleepily at her new community, thinking her long search is at last over.

Then the big shock comes. Loud barking sounds and human voices destroy the silence. The mother runs downward, her nose catching strange smell. A long rope snakes upward and she turns, bares her sharp teeth and puts out her long curves. But her small teddy-bear[1] image is not very scary[2] and does little so discourage the intruders.

Then things happen fast. First, the mother comes crashing downward and is caught by a picture held out below. Her helpless baby offers no challenge, making the rest of the saving easy.

Mother koala and her little one sniff and claw about in the stuffy[3] corn sack as the truck they have been got hold of by Wildlife Management workers, who have orders to drop the orphans off at a small place where they must be left alone for a while. If this is not done, the frightened animals could go into shock and die.

---

[1] teddy-bear *n.* 玩具熊
[2] scary /ˈskɛəri/ *a.* （口语）引起惊慌的；骇人的
[3] stuffy /ˈstʌfi/ *a.* 闷热的；不通气的

醒来后，考拉熊妈妈从头到脚抖了抖毛，将后爪伸进它厚厚的棕色毛皮里进行梳洗，然后用舌头把孩子浑身上下舔洗一遍。做完这一切后，熊妈妈停下来，睡眼朦胧地看着它的新环境，想着它漫长的寻找终于结束了。

紧接着，发生了一件令人震惊的事：响亮的狗叫声和嘈杂的人声打破了沉静。熊妈妈赶紧跑到树下，它的鼻子嗅到了一股怪味。一条长绳在上方吊着。它转过身，露出锋利的牙齿，整个身子呈弯曲形，但它长得像玩具熊，形象并不很吓人，所以没有使那些闯入者气馁。

一切都发生得很快。首先，熊妈妈一下子从树上掉了下来，被下面伸出来的绘有图画的救生垫接住了。它那无助的孩子没有抵抗，这使下面的营救工作变得容易了。

当野生动物管理人员将熊妈妈和它的孩子装进闷热的玉米袋里时，它们大声地喘着气，到处乱抓。那些工人奉命把母子俩放在一个小地方，必须得让它们在那里单独呆一会儿。如不这样做，这些受惊的动物就会因恐惧而死。

After a brief while, the mother gets used to staying in the "quiet place" filled with good eating leaves. But, she isn't used to eating off the floor yet and would still like to have her own tree. Her baby spends much time with her head stuck[1] in the mother's pouch, nursing.

Three days pass before the koalas are once more rounded up[2] and this time put into a wooden car and driven to the zoo hospital for a medical examination.

Mother koala plays as the zoo doctor examines, and even shines lights into her eyes. When it is over the doctor happily reports the five victims are in good health and can be sent to a new koala reserve[3].

Until arrangements are complete, the orphans must stay at the Koala Hilton, an open-face wooden structure, with good eating trees. It is also a popular tourist top-over, which is perfect for visitors to learn something about the country's much-loved animals.

When tourists drop by the hotel, Mother Koala and her baby are brought down from their tree so they can be observed.

---

[1] stick *vi.* 放置
[2] round up 驱拢
[3] reserve /riˈzəːv/ *n.* 禁猎区;专用地

停了一小会儿之后，熊妈妈渐渐习惯了呆在这个充满了好吃树叶的"安静地方"，但它还不习惯在地板上吃，而是喜欢有自己的树。小熊崽好长时间都一直用头顶住熊妈妈的袋子，吃着奶。

三天后，考拉熊又一次被聚拢起来，这次被放到了木车厢里，要运到动物医院里体检。

当动物园医生检查、甚至将灯光照进它的眼睛时，考拉熊妈妈还在玩耍。检查结束，医生高兴地报告说，这五只受灾的熊健康状况良好，可以送到一个新的考拉熊保护区。

一切安排完后，这对孤儿寡母必须呆在考拉熊的希尔顿旅店，这是一个敞开的木结构建筑，有好吃的树，同时也是一个众所周知的旅游胜地，这对旅行者了解这个国家的宠物是再好不过了。

这些旅行者到达旅馆后，考拉熊妈妈和它的孩子们便被从树上带下来，这样人们就可以好好看看了。

Just as the koalas are beginning to like all the good food and attention, the Wildlife Management truck returns with the wooden car. The mother complains as she and her baby are once again driven off. She has no way of knowing that this time there will be a happy ending.

When they reach their new home, the mother run with every tree trunk. Finally, she chooses a tree at the edge of the forest, just like the one they lost in the fire so long ago. They climb higher and higher before stopping at a forked branch close to[1] the top where they sit, stayed together, sleepily gazing over their new neighborhood. Mother koala feels happy and content[2], for she has finally found her good eating tree—a home she and her baby can call their very own.

---

[1] close to 接近于；在附近
[2] content /'kɔntent/ a. 满意的；满足的

　　正当考拉熊们开始喜欢这些食物和人们的关注时,野生动物保护组织带有木制车厢的卡车来了。考拉熊妈妈同它的孩子又一次被带走,这位母亲不太高兴。它不知道这次它将会有一个幸福的结局。

　　当它们到达新家时,熊妈妈到每一棵树干上检查。最后,它在森林边上选了一棵树,就像好久以前它们在森林火灾中失去的那棵树一样。它们越爬越高,一直爬到接近顶端的杈枝上才停下来。它们一起卧在树枝上,懒洋洋地注视着它们的新环境。考拉熊妈妈感到心满意足,因为它最终找到了它喜欢吃的树——它和孩子可以叫作自己家的所在。

The Whitetail

The three deer stepped gracefully through the falling snow. They stood 50 yards from the window of my farmhouse. They looked as if they were

posing for a Christmas card. Then the cold December wind ruffled up[1] their coats. A sea of snow whirled about them. And I saw these beautiful wild beasts for what they really are. Deer are one of the most gentle, yet possibly the toughest, of animals.

The deer looks delicate—with his soft brown eyes, thin limbs and shy ways. But he is strong. The deer survives the terrible winter. He survives in spite of man with his farming, lumbering and road-building, his automobiles and guns.

In spring, summer and fall, the whitetails live almost anywhere. They feed on everything from twigs to wild mushrooms. They have even been seen fishing—pawing suckers from a creek, then eating them head first.

---

[1] ruffle /ˈrʌfl/ up 吹皱

白尾鹿

三只鹿动作优雅地穿过飞扬的落雪,在我农场房屋窗外 50 码以外的地方停下来。它们看上去好像正为拍摄一张圣诞节贺卡摆好姿势。此时,12 月的寒风吹乱了它们的毛皮,它们的周围旋舞着漫天飞雪。我认识了这些美丽的野生动物的真实面目。尽管鹿是一种最温顺的动物,但也可能是最有耐力的动物。

柔和的棕色眼睛、纤细的腿和羞涩的神态使鹿显得娇弱。但它非常强壮。鹿能活过凛冽的寒冬。虽然人们开荒、伐林、修路、开车带枪去捕杀动物,但鹿还是生存了下来。

春夏秋三季几乎在任何地方都可以见到白尾鹿。它们吃一切植物——从嫩树枝到野蘑菇。人们还曾看到过它们捕鱼——它们从小溪中捞起亚口鱼,先从鱼头吃起。

Winter is the hardest season for the whitetails. Then they live mainly on tree and bush growth. They feed on buds, branches and bark. If the snow gets more than two feet deep, the deer "yard". They gather in small groups and trample[1] down the deep snow, making a yard in which they can move about. Whitetails use the same teamwork to open trails after storm. Within 48 hours they pack down the snow so they can travel. But the snows cut down their feeding range. In hard winters many deer starve or die of exposure.

Nature has, however, given the whitetail wonderful equipment to help him survive. For example, his coat helps him blend into the background. His enemies find it hard to spot him.

Also, the whitetail's senses are very sharp. Hunters say that he can detect[2] a flicker of movement or smell a cigarette half a mile away. He also has scent glands to send signals and mark trails. One kind gives off a strong odor to call a baby deer or warn of danger. With another gland, between the toes of each foot, he leaves an odor that helps him retrace[3] his tracks through strange territory.

Whitetail are at home even in water. These deer have been seen paddling more than five miles out in the ocean—just for the fun of it!

---

[1] trample /ˈtræmpl/ vt. 践踏
[2] detect /diˈtekt/ vt. 辨别出
[3] retrace /riˈtreis/ vt. 沿路重行

冬天是白尾鹿最难熬的季节，它们在冬季只能靠树木和灌木为生。它们吃树木的芽苞、枝条和树皮，如果积雪厚度达到两英尺以上，白尾鹿就集居在"鹿场"里。它们一小群一小群地聚在一起，踏平厚厚的积雪，弄成一个围场，好在里边走动。暴风雪过后，白尾鹿用类似的合作方式开辟小路。它们在暴风雪后的48小时内就踏平积雪，这样它们就可以巡游了。尽管如此，大雪还是限制了它们觅食的范围。在特别寒冷多雪的冬日里，常有许多白尾鹿被饿死或冻死。

然而，大自然为白尾鹿提供了极好的装备，帮助它们存活。比如，白尾鹿的皮色使它们和森林融为一体，不易被敌人发现。

白尾鹿还有非常敏锐的感官。据猎人说它能在半英里地以外发现极微小的动静或闻到香烟味。它拥有能发出信号和标下路径的各种香腺。一种香腺能发出强烈的气味，来召唤小鹿或发出危险警报。白尾鹿的另一种味腺位于每只蹄子的足趾之间，在它走过的地方留下气味，帮助自己在陌生的大地上找到回头路。

白尾鹿在水里甚至也是安然自得的。有人看到白尾鹿在大洋里游出去5英里开外——只是为了玩玩！

Whitetail also use water to fight flies and heat—and as a means of escape. An observer once saw a young deer being chased by dogs. The deer doubled back and leaped into a big ditch filled with water. Dogs and men searched and searched. But they could not pick up the deer's trail, so they gave up. Half an hour later, however, the observer noticed faint ripples in the water of the ditch. He leaned over the bank and found the patient little deer. The animal was completely underwater except for nose, forehead and eyes.

The deer has yet another weapon for survival. It is silence. In *The Deer Hunter's Guide*, Mr. Francis E. Sell tells about one of his observations.

Using field glasses[1], Mr. Sell watched a buck crossing an open place in the forest. The ground was cluttered with dry leaves, yet the buck moved silently. How? With each step, the point of his hoof was aimed straight at the ground. Then it was directed a bit forward and placed gently under the leaves. The foot was then brought back, high above the leaves, before it was placed forward again. Later, Mr. Sell studied the deer's path. He found that not a single leaf had been crushed[2]!

---

[1] field glasses 野外双筒望远镜
[2] crush /krʌʃ/ vt. 压碎

白尾鹿还用水来抵御苍蝇和炎热,有时还把水作为逃脱追捕的手段。有人曾看到一头被猎狗追赶的小鹿,这头小鹿返身跑回来一头跃进一条积满了水的沟里。猎狗和猎人反复搜寻,但他们未能找到那只小鹿的踪迹,所以他们只好放弃了追捕。然而,半小时后,那人观察到沟水中泛着涟漪。他从沟岸边探出身子去观察,发现了那只耐心的小鹿。除了鼻子、前额和眼睛,它全身都藏在水里了。

白尾鹿还有另外一种存活的武器,这一武器就是悄无声息。在《猎鹿指南》一书中,弗朗西斯·E·塞尔先生讲述了他观察到的一件事。

塞尔先生用双筒望远镜观察公鹿,一头鹿穿过林间空地,那块土地上到处杂乱地堆积着干树叶。然而,那头鹿却悄然无声地移动着。这是怎样办到的呢?原来那头鹿每迈一步都把蹄尖笔直地对准地面,然后将蹄尖向前伸一点,轻轻地放到树叶底下,接着把蹄子再向后缩回,高高地举起到树叶之上,又向前落下。后来,塞尔显示研究了鹿走过的路。他发现鹿连一片树叶都没踏碎!

Whitetail deer begin mating in November, and a doe usually gives birth to her young in May. There are from one to three babies. The fawns[1] have a red coat with more than 200 spots. These help blend a fawn into its background.

A fawn is able to walk at birth. However, it stays close to the ground, dropping at the slightest noise. Another protection for a newborn deer is that he gives off no scent. Observers have seen dogs jump inches above a fawn without seeing or smelling it.

The doe[2] hides her fawns separately. Then she watches from another places so her scent won't give away her babies. But she stays near enough to lead off any enemies. She has been seen appearing just in time to beat off a fox with her horny hoofs.

Since the doe has very rich milk, her fawns grow rapidly. In 15 days they weigh twice as much as they did at birth. In a month they can eat acorns[3] and beechnuts[4], and at four months they are weaned[5].

---

[1] fawn /fɔːn/ n. 幼鹿
[2] doe /dəu/ 母鹿
[3] acorn /'eikɔːn/ n. 橡子
[4] beechnut /'biːtʃnʌt/ n. 山毛榉坚果
[5] wean /wiːn/ vt. 使断奶

白尾鹿从 11 月份开始交配。母鹿通常在 5 月份产出幼鹿。一胎生一到三头小鹿。幼鹿的红色毛皮上带有 200 多个斑点。这身毛皮使幼鹿和环境浑然一体。

幼鹿生下来就能走，但它们的身子离地面很近；听到一点风吹草动，它们就趴到地上。新生小鹿的另一保护物是它没有任何气味。观察家们曾看到狗从幼鹿身上 8 英寸高的地方跳过，既没看到小鹿，也没闻到小鹿的气味。

母鹿为了防止将自己的气味传给孩子们，便将幼鹿隐藏在别的地方，然后躲开去，从一边看管它们。但它藏身的地方与它的孩子们并不太远，可以及时把敌人引开。人们曾见到母鹿在狐狸接近小鹿时，及时冲出来用它像角一样坚硬的蹄子将狐狸踢跑。

由于母鹿奶水中营养丰富，因此幼鹿成长迅速。幼鹿的体重在出生 15 天后达到出生时的两倍。1 个月后，幼鹿就能吃橡树籽和山毛榉坚果了。到 4 个月大时，幼鹿就断奶了。

leaping deer

At six months some fawns weigh about 125 pounds. If they were the usual youngsters of the wild, they would now he on their own. Not deer. The young bucks stay with the mother for one year, and the does for two.

The deer with his long front legs can make flying leaps, slamming stops, quick turns. I know this from my own experience. One evening last summer I was driving home from a neighbor's. Suddenly a deer came bursting out of the dusk toward my car. I braked to a stop. And so did the deer. But then, from a standstill, he took off. He sailed over the hood of my car with perfect ease. And, with a quick flick of his tail, he disappeared into the night.

Once again I marveled at[1] the deer, beautiful, graceful and tough[2]!

---

[1] marvel /ˈmɑːvəl/ at 对⋯大为惊异
[2] tough /tʌf/ *a.* 坚强的

小母鹿和母亲

有些幼鹿在6个月时体重达到125磅。如果是普通的野生动物的幼兽，现在它们就得独立生活了。鹿却不是这样，小公鹿同母亲在一起生活一年，小母鹿则和母亲一起生活两年。

鹿的前腿极长，可以飞跃而起，在跑动中突然停下来并急速转弯。这是我从自己的经验中了解到的。去年夏天的一个傍晚，我从邻居家开车回家。突然一头鹿冲出暮色，向我的汽车奔来。我刹住车，那头鹿也停住脚步。随后，它从静立状态飞身而起，轻松自如地跃过我的车头，飞快地一甩尾巴，消失在了夜色之中。

我再次为鹿的美丽、优雅和顽强所倾倒。

The Talking Dolphins

Dolphins[1] can make all sorts of sounds. Some scientists believe that these sounds are a language—a way for dolphins to talk to each other. Many scientists are studying these different sounds. They are trying to understand what the sounds mean.

Dolphins make many kinds of sounds. They squeak[2], mew[3], and click[4]. When they are upset or excited they can even yelp[5] like dogs! Most of all, they whistle.

But are they really talking to each other—the way people talk? Or are they only sharing simple feelings and fears—the way other animals, like cats and dogs, do?

---

[1] dolphin /ˈdɔlfin/ n. 海豚
[2] squeak /skwiːk/ vi. 发出短促的尖声
[3] mew /mjuː/ vi. 喵喵叫
[4] click vi. 发出喀哒声
[5] yelp vi. 吠叫

对话海豚

海豚可以发出各种各样的声音。一些科学家认为,这些声音是一种语言——是海豚之间相互交流的一种方式。很多科学家正在研究这些不同的声音,他们试图了解这些声音意味着什么。

海豚可以发出好多种不同的声音,它们可以发出短促的尖叫声、喵喵的叫声和咔哒咔哒的声音。当它们忐忑不安或情绪激动时,甚至能像狗那样吠叫!在大多数情况下,它们发出的是哨声。

但它们彼此真的能谈话——能像人那样交谈吗?要么是它们像其他动物那样只传递一些简单的感觉或恐惧,就像猫和狗那样?

Dr. Jarvis Bastian decided to find out. He worked with two dolphins named Doris and Buzz. Then Dr. Bastian got an old automobile[1] headlight. This light would help him with his tests. Sometimes Dr. Bastian turned on the light and let it shine without going off. This meant "push the right-hand button." Sometimes he let the light shine on and off. Then Doris and Buzz were supposed to[2] push their left-hand button instead.

Before long Dorsi and Buzz learned to watch the light. They pushed down the correct button with their own noses. Then Dr. Bastian gave them their reward—a piece of fish.

Dr. Bastian made the test harder. The dolphins still had to watch the light and push down the correct button. But now Dorsi had to wait. Buzz had to push his button first. Then it was Doris's turn. If she pushed her buttons first, neither of them got any fish.

At first Doris and Buzz made a few minutes. But soon they learned how to do this too. Now it was time for the last and most important part of the test.

---

[1] automobile /ˈɔːtəməubiːl, ˌɔːtəˈməubil, ˌɔːtəməˈbiːl/ n. 汽车
[2] be supposed /səˈpəuzd/ to 应该

加威斯·巴斯蒂安博士决定搞个水落石出。他跟两只海豚在一块工作,一只名叫多丽丝,一只名叫伯斯。巴斯蒂安博士买了一盏旧汽车前灯,这个灯可以帮助他做实验。有时,巴斯蒂安博士扭开灯,让它一直亮着。这就意味着"按右边的按钮"。有时,他让灯一会儿亮一会儿灭。随后,多丽丝和伯斯就应该去按它们左边的按钮。

很快,多丽丝和伯斯学会了观察灯。它们用自己的鼻子去按下正确的按钮。于是,巴斯蒂安教授就会赏给它们一块鱼肉。

巴斯蒂安教授又加大了试验的难度。两只海豚仍然必须观察灯,按动正确的按钮。但现在多丽丝必须等待,伯斯必须先按钮,然后才轮到多丽丝。如果多丽丝先按动按钮,它们俩谁也得不到鱼。

最初,多丽丝和伯斯等了几分钟。但过了不久,它们就学会了怎么做到这一点。现在实验到了最后的阶段,也是最重要的阶段。

Dr. Bastian put a wooden wall across the pool. Doris and her two buttons were on one side of the wall. Buzz and his two buttons were on the other side. But only Doris could see the light. Only she could see if it was shining without going off, or if it was going on and off. But Doris had to wait for Buzz to push his button before she could push hers.

What would the dolphins do? Dr. Bastian turned on the light and watched carefully. Doris stared at it. She looked at her buttons. Then she swam close to the wooden wall and began to whistle loudly. For a few seconds everything was quiet in the tank. Then Buzz whistled back and pushed down one of his buttons. It was the correct one. Now Doris could push her button. Then both of them would get their fish.

Again and again Dr. Bastian turned on the light. Sometimes it shone on and off. Sometimes it shone without going off. Each time Doris would look and whistle. Then Buzz would push down the correct button on his side of the wall.

Was Doris telling what to do? Or was he just guessing? If so, Dr. Bastian thought, then Buzz could guess very well. Buzz was right almost every time.

巴斯蒂安教授在水池里设了一堵木墙。多丽丝和它的两个按钮在一边的墙上，伯斯和它的两个按钮在另一边的墙上。但只有多丽丝能看见灯光，只有它能看见灯是否一直亮着，或者是一会儿亮一会灭。但多丽丝必须等到伯斯按动按钮，它才能按自己的按钮。

海豚会怎么做呢？巴斯蒂安教授打开灯，认真观察。多丽丝凝视着灯，看着按钮，然后游到木墙跟前，开始大声吹哨。好几秒钟，水池里一片安静。尔后，伯斯吹起了口哨，并按下它的一个按钮，那是个正确的按钮。现在多丽丝可以按它这边的按钮了。它们俩都吃到了鱼。

巴斯蒂安教授一遍又一遍地开灯，有时灯开了又关，有时灯一直亮着。每次多丽丝都是先看灯，再吹口哨，然后伯斯就在它那边按动那个正确的按钮。

多丽丝是在告诉伯斯怎么做吗？要么说伯斯是在猜测？如果是猜测，巴斯蒂安教授认为，伯斯猜得恰到好处。伯斯几乎每次都猜对了。

Flying Blaze

Billy was a boy who loved horses more than anything else in the world. He loved his own pony[1], Blaze, best of all. After his father and mother gave him Blaze, Billy spent most of his time with the pony. Blaze would come whenever Billy called. He seemed to like the rides through the woods or along the roads as much as Billy did.

Billy felt sure that Blaze understood him when he talked. And the pony really did seem to know what Billy said.

Billy's dog, Rex, usually went with them on their rides. But one day Rex was sick, so Billy's mother kept him at home.

It was a beautiful day, and Billy decided to ride along a little road that passed through some woods. Both Billy and Blaze liked to ride through the woods because there were so many things to see. They always met rabbits and squirrels[2] and saw many birds. Flowers grew along the way, and the big trees were green and cool after the hot, dusty[3] roads. The summer had been very warm, and there had been little rain.

---

[1] pony /ˈpəuni/ n. 小马
[2] squirrel /ˈskwirəl/ n. 松鼠
[3] dusty a. 满是灰尘的

飞马火焰

比利是一个爱马胜过世界上其他一切的男孩。他最爱自己那匹脸上有白斑的小马——布莱兹。比利的父母亲将布莱兹送给他之后,他大部分时间都跟那匹小马在一起。无论比利什么时候呼喊布莱兹,它都会应声而至。它似乎像比利那样喜欢穿过森林或沿着大路行走。

比利敢肯定,他说话时,布莱兹能够听懂。小马似乎对比利所说的话真的心领神会。

比利的狗莱克斯通常跟他们一路同行。但有一天,莱克斯病了。于是,比利的母亲就把狗留在了家里。

那天风和日丽,所以比利决定骑着布莱兹沿着一条穿林而过的小路前行。比利和布莱兹都喜欢那样做,因为沿途有好多值得看的东西。他们总会碰见野兔和松鼠,还会看到好多小鸟。沿途鲜花盛开,大树在热浪逼人、布满灰尘的路上覆盖上了绿荫,凉爽宜人。那个夏天十分炎热,而且干旱少雨。

They had gone quite a long way when Blaze suddenly stopped. Billy looked ahead and saw smoke coming out of a pile of dry brush at the side of the road. He knew that it was against the law to build fires in the woods during the dry season. It was not a safe thing to do because there was the danger of starting[1] a forest fire.

Even as Billy looked, the flames burst out. He knew that these flames were the beginning of a forest fire unless they could be put out. If a breeze[2] came up and carried the fire to the big pine trees near by, the whole countryside might burn. Not only the grass and trees would be burned, fences and barns and horses and houses would also go up in flames.

Billy had once seen a place where there had been a forest fire. He remembered how bare and black it had looked, with burned stumps[3] where beautiful trees had been. He knew he must try to save the woods he loved so much. He must go quickly and get help.

---

[1] start　*vt.* 发动；起动
[2] breeze /briːz/　*n.* 微风
[3] stump　*n.* 树桩；残余

他们走了好长一段路，布莱兹突然停住脚步。比利向前望去，只见从路边的一堆干灌木丛中冒出烟来。他知道旱季在森林里生火是违法的。这样做很不安全，因为有引发森林大火的危险。

　　就在比利看着的当儿，火焰呼地蹿出。他知道，这些火焰要是不被扑灭，将会是森林大火的开始。假如刮来一阵微风将火吹到附近的那些大松树上，整个林区都可能会燃烧起来。不仅草和树会燃烧，而且篱笆、谷仓、马和房子也会腾起火焰。

　　比利曾见过一个地方发生过森林大火。他记得整个林区都黑乎乎、光秃秃的，漂亮的树木只剩下了烧过的树桩。他知道他必须设法拯救自己打心眼里喜爱的这片森林。他必须立马行动去求救。

火灾后的森林

The nearest place to go for help was a large farm. It was a long way to this farm by the road, and there was no time to lose. Billy knew they could save much time if they cut across country through the fields. But to reach the first field they would have to jump a high stone wall. It was higher than anything Blaze had ever jumped. But Blaze seemed to understand that they needed to hurry. He jumped the high wall perfectly.

Then they went on as fast as they could across the wide field. Billy did not need to coax[1] Blaze. The pony was going like the wind. If he could only keep up this speed, they would soon reach the farmhouse.

In the middle of the field was a river. There was no bridge and no time to look for a shallow place to cross. "Come on, Blaze," called Billy, and Blaze went even faster than before.

The nearer they came to the river, the wider it seemed. It was too late to stop now. They were right at the water's edge. Blaze made a big leap. Billy could feel how hard he was trying. It seemed that they would surely get over the river safely.

As they landed, the bank gave way[2] under Blaze's hind feet. For a moment Billy thought they would fall back into the brook. But Blaze scrambled[3] up the bank. Then they were off as fast as the pony could go.

---

[1] coax /kəuks/ vt. 耐心使…；哄
[2] give way 让路；后退
[3] scramble /ˈskræmbl/ vi. 爬行；攀缘

离得最近的求救点是一家大农场。沿着大路去这个农场得走好长一段路，现在一分一秒都不能耽搁。比利知道，他们要是穿越几块田地，能省好多时间。但要到达第一块田地，他们必须跳过一堵高高的石墙。布莱兹还从来没跳过这样高的障碍，但它似乎明白他们需要抓紧时间，于是就动作完美地跃过了那堵高墙。

随后，他们尽可能快地越过那块广阔的田野。比利不必去哄布莱兹。小马正在像一阵风似地飞奔着。只要它能够一直保持这个速度，他们很快就会赶到那家农舍。

一条河从田野中间横穿而过。河上没有桥，也来不及寻找一个水浅的地方涉水渡河。"快，布莱兹，"比利喊道。之后，布莱兹比以前跑得更快了。

他们离得越近，河好像变得越宽。他们已经到了河边，停下来已经来不及了。布莱兹纵身一跃。比利能感觉到小马在用多大的劲儿。看上去他们一定会安然无恙地越过河去。

就在他们落地之际，布莱兹的后蹄一下子把河岸压塌了。刹那间，比利想着他们会跌落河里，但布莱兹爬上了河岸。接着，他们便马不停蹄飞驰而去。

Blaze was breathing hard now, but the farmhouse was near.

Suddenly, Billy pulled Blaze to a stop. There, right in front of them, was a high wall with barbed wire[1] at the top. He looked both ways but there was no gate in sight. Billy almost gave up, but the thought of the fire sweeping across the countryside was too much. They must go on.

"Just once more, Blaze," he whispered to the pony. Poor Blaze was very tired, but he galloped bravely toward the fence. He was straining every muscle for the jump.

They were almost over when Billy felt Blaze's hind legs catch on the wire, and they began to fall. Down went Blaze to his knees, and Billy slipped out of the saddle[2] and up to the pony's neck.

It seemed certain that Blaze would go down all the way, taking Billy with him. But, with a great effort, Blaze scrambled to his feet. And Billy, holding onto the pony's neck, stayed on. Then Blaze started at a gallop[3] for the farmhouse just across the field.

---

[1] barbed wire （美）带刺铁丝网
[2] saddle /ˈsædl/ n. 鞍
[3] gallop /ˈgæləp/ vi. 疾驰；飞奔

布莱兹此时气喘吁吁,但农舍就在不远处。

突然,比利将布莱兹勒住,因为他们的正前方是一堵高墙,墙头拦着有刺铁丝网。他左右看了看,但看不见大门。比利正要放弃,但一想到大火就要席卷整个林区,他就心急如焚。他们必须继续前进。

"请再跃一次,布莱兹,"他对小马低声说。可怜的布莱兹确实很累了,但它又勇敢地向那篱笆墙疾驰而去,绷紧每一块肌肉飞身起跳。

就在他们差不多要过去的当儿,比利感到布莱兹的后腿绊住了铁丝。他们开始跌落。当布莱兹跪倒时,比利滑离马鞍,扑到了布莱兹的脖子上。

好像布莱兹驮着比利要完全栽倒在地,但布莱兹竭尽全力,又爬着站了起来。比利紧紧地抱住布莱兹的脖颈,没有跌落下来。接着,布莱兹开始向田野对面的那个农舍飞驰而去。

They galloped into the farmyard. The farmer and his son hurried over to meet Billy. All out of breath, he told them about the fire. At once they got some things to use in putting it out. Then the farmer and his son climbed into a car and drove off very fast. The farmer's wife telephoned to the neighbors to send all the help they could. By acting quickly they would be able to put out the fire before any real harm was done.

The barbed wire had cut Blaze's legs. So the farmer's wife brought warm water and medicine and helped Billy wash the cuts clean and bandage them. They were not deep cuts, and the farmer's wife said she was sure they would be better soon.

Blaze was covered with sweat and dirt. He was a very tired pony, but he rubbed his nose against Billy. He seemed to know that the boy was proud of him.

"You're the best pony in the world, Blaze—the very best!" said Billy, and he felt sure that what he said was true.

他们奔进那家农舍。农场主和他的儿子赶忙过来迎接比利。比利气喘吁吁地把失火的情况告诉了他们。他们立马取来了灭火器具。随后,农场主和儿子钻进一辆汽车,呼啸而去。农场主的妻子给左邻右舍打电话,让他们全力去救火。由于行动迅速,因此他们一定能在酿成真正的损失之前扑灭大火。

刺铁丝网划破了布莱兹的腿。于是,农场主的妻子端过温水,取来药物,帮助比利清洗和包扎小马腿上的伤口。伤口划得不深。农场主的妻子说,她敢肯定伤口不久就会好起来的。

布莱兹满身汗水和灰土。它已经筋疲力尽,但它的鼻子还是在比利身上擦来擦去。它似乎知道这个男孩为他感到骄傲。

"你是世界上最棒的小马,布莱兹——绝对最棒!"比利说,而且他确信自己说的没错。

Spaceship Under the Apple Tree

One summer night just before he went to bed, Eddie stood in his grandmother's yard looking up at the star-filled sky.

"There are lots of shooting stars[1] out tonight, Grandmother," he said.

"Why don't you make a wish, Eddie?" asked his grandmother.

"Oh, Grandmother," said Eddie. "I don't wish on shooting stars. They are really great meteors[2] burning out there in space. If they don't burn out, they fall to earth and make big holes. Look, one just went over the hill close to[3] the apple orchard[4]!"

"My[5]! My!" said his grandmother. "It might have come down on top of Grandfather's apple tree. If I were to make a wish on that star, I'd just wish it didn't come down to earth."

Grandfather's big apple tree was the oldest tree in the orchard.

---

[1] shooting star *n.* 流星
[2] meteor /ˈmiːtiə(r)/ *n.* 流星
[3] close to 离…很近
[4] orchard /ˈɔːtʃəd/ *n.* 果园
[5] my *int.* 哎呀

苹果树下的太空飞船

一个夏夜，上床睡觉之前，埃迪站在奶奶的院子里，抬头望着繁星满天的夜空。

"奶奶，今天晚上有好多流星，"他说。

"埃迪，你何不许个愿呢？"奶奶问道。

"噢，奶奶，"埃迪说，"我不会对流星许愿的。它们其实是在太空中快要燃尽的大流星。如果燃不尽，它们就会落在地球上，砸出大窟窿的。瞧，其中一颗落在了苹果园附近的小山那边！"

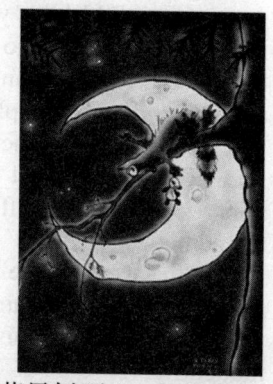

"哎呀！哎呀！"奶奶说，"它可能落到了爷爷的苹果树顶上。如果我对那颗星星许个愿，我只愿它不要落到地球上。"

爷爷的大苹果树是苹果园里最老的一棵树。

"I guess it didn't come down on Grandfather's tree. But I wish a real meteor would come down around here somewhere," said Eddie. "Just a little one, Grandmother, one that wouldn't hurt anything. It wouldn't hurt anything if it came down in the road."

"Well, no stars will be coming down just by wishing them down," said his grandmother. "It's getting late, Eddie, so you'd better go to bed. But I'd like to have you go up to the orchard the first thing tomorrow morning. I'm a little bit worried about Grandfather's apple tree."

"O.K., Grandmother. I'll go up to the orchard," said Eddie. "But don't worry about that meteor. I think it's shooting off into space. Good night, Grandmother."

Eddie went up the stairs two at a time, took a running jump, and landed on his bed. Then he pulled off one of his shoes and stopped and thought...

What if the meteor really did come down in the apple orchard? What if it had struck Grandfather's apple tree? What if it were up there right now burning and burning? What did it look like burning away like that?

"My job tomorrow morning is to go up to the apple orchard for Grandmother," Eddie told himself as he slowly took off his other shoe. Suddenly he thought...

But why wait until morning? If that old meteor landed, it's burning right now.

"我想它不会落到爷爷的树上的。但我希望一颗真正的流星会落到这里附近的某个地方,"埃迪说,"奶奶,就小小的一颗,不会伤害任何东西的一颗。如果它落在路上,就不会伤害任何东西。"

"噢,哪颗行星也不会按希望的那样落下来,"他奶奶说,"埃迪,天越来越晚了,所以你最好上床睡觉去吧。但我想让你明天早上首先去苹果园。我有点儿担心你爷爷的那棵苹果树。"

"奶奶,行。我会去苹果园的,"埃迪说,"但别为那颗流星担心。我想它要飞到太空中去了。奶奶,晚安。"

埃迪一次上两级楼梯,一蹦一跳,躺到了他的床上。随后,他脱掉一只鞋,停下来,沉思起来……

如果流星真的落在苹果怎么办?如果它真砸着爷爷的苹果树怎么办?如果它一直在那里燃烧怎么办?它那样燃烧会是什么样子呢?

"我明天早上的任务是替奶奶到苹果园去,"埃迪一边慢腾腾地脱另一只鞋,一边自言自语说。突然,他想了起来……

但为什么要等到明天早上呢?如果那颗老流星落下来,它马上就会燃烧的。

He heard his grandmother's bedroom door close. He thought another minute or two. Then he quietly slipped out of his bedroom window. He slid down from the balcony[1] to the ground below.

The moon threw shadows of the leaves and branches on the earth. The whole ground looked as if it were covered with a fine carpet.

Soon Eddie could see the old tree and its shadow. There was no sign of a fallen meteor. At first there seemed nothing different about the old tree.

Then Eddie saw something that made his hair stand up straight!

On a big branch of the old tree, about ten feet up from the ground, something moved! It was a little man!

The little man was on the branch, but he was not on the topside of it. He stood on the underside as if his feet were pasted there! He wore a strange green suit.

The little man was about three feet tall. He seemed to be looking out over the countryside with a tiny telescope. Suddenly he felt like a shot, head first from the branch! He landed with a bang on his head. As he stood up he saw Eddie.

"Speak...English?" he asked in a high voice.

"Yes...I do," answered Eddie slowly.

---

[1] balcony /'bælkəni/ n. 阳台

他听到奶奶的卧室门关上了。他又想了一两分钟，随后悄悄地从他卧室的窗户溜出来，从阳台滑到了下面的地上。

月亮将树叶和树枝的阴影投到了地上，整个地面看上去像是铺了一块漂亮的地毯。

埃迪很快就看到了那棵老苹果树和它的影子。没有流星落下的迹象。起先看上去好像老苹果树没有什么两样。

后来，埃迪看到了让他毛骨悚然的东西！

在距离地面大约有 10 英尺的老苹果树的一条大枝上有个东西在动！是个小人儿！

那个小人儿站在树枝上，但他不是站在树枝上面，而是站在树枝下面，好像他的两只脚粘到了上面！他穿着一身奇怪的绿衣服。

那个小人儿大约有 3 英尺高。他好像在通过小小的望远镜眺望着乡村。突然，他感到好像中弹一样，头朝下从树枝上摔了下来！他的头咚的一声撞在地上。当他站起来时，看到了埃迪。

"说……英语吗？"他高声问道。

"是的……我会说，"埃迪慢慢地答道。

"Good," said the little man. "One minute, please." He pulled a small box out of a pocket in his short coat. He opened it with a key. In the box were envelopes filled with cards. He looked at the writing on one card and said, "You...are...born in America?"

"Yes," said Eddie.

"Good," said the little man. "One minute." He looked in another envelope.

Eddie began to get over his first surprise. "Look here!" he said in a loud, angry voice. "What's going on here?"

As Eddie talked the little man stopped looking through his shining box of cards. He suddenly touched Eddie's arm with one of his fingers.

Eddie sat down hard on the ground!

"Speak slowly," said the little man.

Eddie got to his feet. His fingers closed into fists. He raised his fists.

The little man held out his finger. "I come from the planet Martinea."

Eddie took a big breath. Then he remembered what he had read in books. "Martinea?" he said. "The planet Martinea? There's no such planet!"

The little man looked into his box again.

"What's that box?" asked Eddie.

"This box gives me key to English," said the little man. "Our people learn English through telescopes from Martinea."

"How could they?" asked Eddie.

"好,"那个小人儿说,"请等一会儿。"他从短大衣口袋里掏出一个小盒子,用钥匙打开。盒子是装满卡片的信封。他看到其中一张上面写道:"你……出生……在美国吗?"

"是的,"埃迪说。

"好,"那个小人儿说,"等一下。"他向另一个信封里看。

埃迪渐渐战胜了当初的吃惊。"看这里!"他用洪亮的声音生气地说,"这里发生了什么事儿?"

埃迪说话时,那个小人儿不再看他那闪亮的卡片盒。他突然用一根手指抚摸埃迪的胳膊。

埃迪扑通一声坐在了地上!

"慢慢说,"那个小人儿说。

埃迪站起来,手指握成拳头,举了起来。

那个小人儿伸出手指,说:"我是从马丁尼星来的。"

埃迪大喘了一口气,随后想起了他在书上看到的事情。"马丁尼?"他说,"马丁尼星?没有这样一个星星!"

那个小人儿又向他的盒子里看了看。

"那只盒子是什么?"埃迪问。

"这只盒子给了我学习英语的钥匙,"那个小人儿说,"我们的人是通过马丁尼星上的望远镜学习英语的。"

"那怎么可能呢?"埃迪问。

"We see through telescopes your English on highways—'Steep hill! Turn left! Safety first!' We learn English from signs."

"Where's Martinea?" Eddie asked.

The little man pointed toward the moon.

"Martinea far away from your sun," he said. "We see the earth through telescopes."

"Well, I never heard of it," said Eddie. "If you did come from this far planet Martinea, how did you get here?"

The little man looked at Eddie as if he were making up his mind. Then he said, "Come, I show you."

He turned and walked over the hill back of Grandfather's apple tree. Eddie followed. About ten feet from the tree trunk, the little man jerked away a lot of branches, that covered something.

In a few minutes the moonlight showed something which looked like a giant overturned[1] dish.

"A Flying Saucer!" shouted Eddie. "No, it can't be! There are no such things as Flying Saucers!"

The little man turned to Eddie, and quickly opened his box again.

"F...F...Flying..." he said as he flipped through the cards. "There are no Flying Saucers."

"Sure," said Eddie. "There are no Flying Saucers. I read it in a book."

---

[1] overturned /ˌəuvəˈtəːnd/ *a.* 颠倒的

"我们通过望远镜看你们写在公路上的英语单词——'陡山！向左拐！安全第一！'我们是通过这些标志学习英语的。"

"马丁尼星在什么地方？"埃迪问。

那个小人儿向月亮那边指了指。

"马丁尼星距离你们的太阳很远，"他说，"我们通过望远镜可以看到你们的地球。"

"噢，我从来没有听说过这种事，"埃迪说，"如果你真是从那颗遥远的马丁尼星上下来的，那你是怎么到达这里的呢？"

那个小人儿看着埃迪，好像在下决心似的。随后，他说："过来，我给你看。"

他转过来，走过爷爷的苹果树后面的小山丘。埃迪跟在后面。在距离树干大约10英尺的地方，那个小人儿猛地拽下了好多树枝，这些树枝原来遮住了一些东西。

过了一会儿，月光照出了看上去像一只翻转过来的巨大碟子的什么东西。

"飞碟！"埃迪大声叫道，"不，这是不可能的！没有飞碟这样的东西！"

那个小人儿转向埃迪，然后又飞快地打开他的盒子。

"飞……飞……飞……"他一边翻着卡片，一边说，"没有飞碟。"

"当然，"埃迪说，"没有飞碟。我在一本书上看过的。"

"This is a Spaceship." said the little man, and he began to cover his spaceship again. "No Flying Saucers!"

When he finished covering the spaceship, he turned to Eddie.

"Tell me," he said. "Where is place for pilot to rest? Must wait for this side of earth to turn to sun."

"You mean daylight?" said Eddie.

"Yes, daylight," said the little man.

"If you want to rest, come down to my grandmother's house," said Eddie. "She won't mind...I think."

"Let's go," said the little man.

Eddie found himself obeying the little man. Through the orchard they both raced to Eddie's grandmother house.

"这是太空飞船,"那个小人儿说,然后又盖住了他的太空飞船。"没有飞碟!"

盖好太空飞船后,他转向埃迪。

"告诉我,"他说,"让飞行员休息的地方在哪里?必须等到地球这面转到太阳那边吗?"

"你是说白天吧?"埃迪说。

"是的,白天,"那个小人儿说。

"如果你想休息,就到我奶奶的房子里来吧,"埃迪说,"她不会介意的……我想。"

"我们走吧,"那个小人儿说。

Was it the sun shining into his window or his grandmother's voice that woke him the next morning? As he lay there half-awake he thought…Dreams are good things. A fellow can have more adventure with his eyes closed than he can when they're wide open. Dream about flying…dream about…

After a minute or two his grandmother called up from the kitchen again.

"Eddie, remember your promise. You said you would go up to the orchard."

Eddie's eyes flashed open. That's what he had dreamed about, going up to the orchard! Or did he dream it? Eddie sat up in his bed as he remembered the little man. Quickly he looked around the room. There was no sign of the little man

"What a dream that was!" said Eddie.

埃迪发现自己非常听那个小人儿的话。他们俩飞快地穿过苹果园，向埃迪奶奶的房子走去。

第二天早上，不知是照进他的窗户的太阳光还是他奶奶把他叫醒的呢？当半睡半醒躺在那里时，他想……做梦真是一件好事。一个人合上眼体验到的冒险比他睁开眼所体验到的还要多。梦见飞行……梦见有关……

一两分钟后，他奶奶又在厨房叫他。

"埃迪，记住你的诺言。你说过要去果园的。"

埃迪睁开了眼睛。去果园，那正是他梦想到的东西！或者说他梦到的是果园吗？当想起那个小人儿时，埃迪从被窝里坐了起来。他飞快地扫视房间四周，没有小人儿的踪影。

"那梦真美！"埃迪说。

Grandpa at Sea

The summer I was seven was a very happy time for me. That summer Grandpa showed me how to row a boat. "I want you to make friends with the sea," he said.

Grandpa's house was right by the sea, in Maine. Winds often pushed the sea into big waves. The waves came up almost to the rocks in front of the house.

At those times, Grandpa said, "Come along, Davy. Let's go meet the sea!"

We climbed down over the big rocks together. At times, we went too near the water. Then a wave would knock us down.

I cried the first time this happened. "I'm afraid!" I said.

But Grandpa said, "Come along now! You must learn not to be afraid."

How brave Grandpa seemed to me! I wanted to be like him.

Most men in the town were fishermen. They set out lobster traps[1] in the sea.

An old fisherman named Al let us use his boat. Al's strong, heavy boat road the waves well.

Al was very poor. But he would not take money for the boat from Grandpa.

---

[1] lobster /ˈlɔbstə(r)/ trap =lobster pot 龙虾笼

跟着爷爷出海

7岁那年夏天对我来说是一段幸福的时光。那年夏天,爷爷教会了我怎样划船。"我想让你和大海成为朋友,"他说。

爷爷的房子就座落在缅因州的海边。海风经常将大海掀起大浪。海浪几乎吹到房前的岩石边。

当时,爷爷说:"戴维,跟我来。让我们去迎接大海吧!"

我们一块爬过那些大岩石,不时地走近水边。随后,一个海浪常常将我们掀翻。

第一次发生这种事时,我哭了起来。"我害怕!"我说。

但爷爷说:"快来吧!你必须学会怎样不害怕。"

在我看来,爷爷是多么勇敢啊!我想跟他一样。

镇上的大多数男人都是渔夫。他们在大海里放下龙虾笼。

一个名叫奥尔的老渔夫让我们用他的船。奥尔坚固的大船迎风破浪,运行良好。

奥尔很穷,但他不愿收爷爷的船钱。

Grandpa found another way to pay him. He knew that Al had to make his lobster traps from old wood. These traps always came to pieces in a storm. So Grandpa made Al some fine lobster traps from new wood.

Al liked his new traps very much. He showed them to all the fishermen. Then he set them out in the water.

One day, there was a very big storm, Grandpa and I went down to the sea. The men were standing around, talking. But Al was not with them.

"Where is Al?" Grandpa asked.

"Out there in his boat," one man said. He pointed to the sea. "He's trying to get those traps you made for him. But he lost an oar[1]. He can't get back."

"We must go out and tow[2] him in," Grandpa said. "Who will go with me?"

No one answered. Who wanted to go to sea in such a bad storm?

Grandpa walked to a boat. "I'll go with you, Grandpa!" I said, jumping into the boat beside him.

Grandpa started to tell me not to come. Then he picked up the heavy oars. He pushed us out into the deep water.

---

[1] oar /ɔː(r)/ n. 船桨
[2] tow /təʊ/ vt. 拖；拽

爷爷找到了另一个为他付钱的方法。他知道奥尔不得不用旧木头做龙虾笼。这些笼子总是在暴风雨中被击成碎片。因此,爷爷就用新木头为奥尔做了一些耐用的龙虾笼。

奥尔非常喜欢这些新笼子。他把这些笼子给所有的渔夫们看;然后,他将笼子放进水中。

一天,起了大风暴,我和爷爷去海边。那些人站成一圈,谈论着。但奥尔没有和他们在一起。

"奥尔在哪里?"爷爷问道。

"在外边他的船里,"其中一个人说。他指向大海。"他在设法收回你为他做的那些笼子。但他丢了一只船桨,无法回来了。"

"我们必须出海把他救回来,"爷爷说,"谁愿意和我一块去?"

没有人回答。谁想在暴风骤雨中出海呢?

爷爷向一条船走去。"爷爷,我愿意和你一起去!"我说着,跳进他身边的那条船里。

爷爷开始不让我去。随后,他拿起了沉重的船桨,将我们推进了深水区。

Grandpa was standing in the boat. He had lost his hat. His white hair was blowing in the wind. He turned and smiled at me. At that very minute, I stopped being afraid.

Grandpa pulled on the oars. The waves were high. With each wave, the boat went up in the air. Then it banged[1] down on the water. Up, down, up, down we went.

From the top of a wave, we saw Al. He was trying to use his one oar. But water was filling his boat. Could we get to him in time?

---

[1] bang /bæŋ/ vi. 撞

　爷爷站在船里。他已经把帽子丢了。他的白发在风中飘动着。他转过身，向我微微一笑。此时此刻，我不再感到害怕了。

　爷爷划着桨。海浪高涨。船随着每一个波浪荡向空中，随后又咚的一声落进了浪底。我们上下颠簸着向前行进。
　我们从浪峰顶端看到了奥尔。他正在设法用一只船桨划行。但水正在往他的小船里灌。我们能及时赶到他那里吗？

Yes! Soon Grandpa pulled near enough for Al to throw us a tow rope. We tied the rope to our boat. Then Grandpa began rowing back to land.

Big waves followed us in. One of them made Al's heavy boat hit our light one. I thought both boats would sink.

Then Grandpa turned our boat around! Were we going back to sea?

"We'll have to back[1] in, Davy," Grandpa said. "Then Al's boat will be in front us. It can't hit us."

The waves still came at us, pushing us to land. But now they pushed Al's boat away from us. Al got to land first.

At last we climbed out onto the bank. One fisherman hurried to put a coat around Grandpa.

Al came over to shake Grandpa's hand. He knew how brave Grandpa had been. So did I. But Grandpa just said, "Come on. Davy, let's go home!"

---

[1] back vi. 后退；倒退

是的！爷爷马上就划到了近旁，让奥尔将拖绳扔给了我们。我们将拖绳绑到了我们的船上。随后，爷爷开始往陆地上划。

大浪一个接一个地跟着我们。其中一个大浪使奥尔的重船撞在了我们的轻船上。我以为两艘船都会沉没的。

随后，爷爷便将我们的船转了过来！我们要返回大海吗？

"戴维，我们必须得退回去，"爷爷说，"这样奥尔的船就会到我们前面了。他就不会撞我们了。"

海浪仍在向我们袭来，将我们推向陆地。但它们现在将奥尔的船推离了我们。奥尔首先到达了陆地。

最后，我们爬到了岸上。其中有一名渔夫赶忙用一件大衣裹住了爷爷。

奥尔走过来握着爷爷的手。他知道爷爷是多么勇敢。我也知道。但爷爷只是说："快点儿，戴维，我们回家去吧！"

Feathered Friend

"I'm going nuts[1] here by myself," Pat Myers confessed to her daughter, Annie. Pat had been virtually confined to her house for a year as she was treated for an inflamed artery in her temple that affected her vision and stamina[2].

A widow with two married children, she'd been happily running a chain of dress shops. But now that she had to give up her business, her home began to feel oppressively silent and empty. Finally she admitted to Annie how lonely she was.

"Do you think I should advertise for someone to live with me?"

"That's such a gamble," Annie said. "How about a pet?"

"I haven't the strength to walk a dog," Pat said. "I'm allergic[3] to cats, and fish don't have a whole lot to say."

"Birds do," said her daughter. "Why not get a parrot?" And so it began.

---

[1] go nuts 发疯
[2] stamina /'stæminə/ n. 精力；耐力
[3] allergic /ə'lə:dʒik/ a. 过敏的

有羽毛的朋友

"我一个人呆得要发疯了,"帕特·迈尔斯对女儿安妮坦言。帕特太阳穴处一条动脉发炎,这影响了她的视力和精力。接受治疗一年来,事实上,她一直被关在房子里。

她是一个寡妇,身边有两个结婚成家的孩子,一直开心地经营着几家服装连锁店。但由于她不得不放弃生意呆在家里,因此渐渐感觉沉闷空寂。最后,她向安妮承认她好寂寞。

"你觉得是不是我应该招聘个人来跟我一起生活呢?"

"那太冒险,"安妮说,"养个宠物怎么样?"

"我可没劲儿去遛狗,"帕特说,"我对猫又反感,而鱼根本不会说话。"

"鸟会说话,"女儿说,"干嘛不养只鹦鹉呢?"于是事情就这样定了。

Pat and Annie visited a breeder of African Greys and were shown two little featherless creatures huddled together for warmth. Pat was doubtful, but Annie persuaded her to put a deposit[1] down on the bird with the bright eyes. When he was three months old and feathered out, he was delivered to his new owner, who named him Casey.

A few weeks later Pat told Annie, "I didn't realize I talked so much. Casey's picking up all kinds of words."

"I told you." Her daughter smiled at the sound of pleasure in Pat's voice.

The first sentence Casey learned was "Where's my glasses?" followed by "Where's my purse?" Whenever Pat began scanning tabletops and opening drawers, Casey chanted, "Where's my glasses? Where's my purse?" When she returned from an errand, he'd greet her with, "Holy smokes[2], it's cold out there," in a perfect imitation of her voice.

Casey disliked being caged, so Pat often let him roam the house. "What fun it is to have him," she told Annie. "It makes the whole place feel better."

"I think you're beginning to feel better too," said Annie.

"Well, he gives me four or five laughs a day—they say laughter's good for you."

---

[1] deposit /di'pɔzit / n. 保证金；押金
[2] Holy smokes 表示惊讶或气愤等，意为"哟"

帕特和安妮走访了一名非洲灰鸟的饲养员，见到了两只挤在一起取暖的没有羽毛的小东西。帕特拿不准要还是不要，但安妮还是说服她为那只长有一双明亮眼睛的鸟交了定金。小鸟三个月大时，长出了羽毛，被送到了它的新主人那里，主人给它取名叫凯西。

几周后，帕特对安妮说："我原来没意识到我会说那么多。凯西慢慢学会说各种各样的话了。"

"我说的没错吧。"女儿听到帕特话语里愉快的声音，露出了微笑。

凯西学说的第一句话是"我的眼镜哪去了？"接着是"我的钱包呢？"逢到帕特开始扫视桌面，继而拉开抽屉，凯西便会一再说："我的眼镜哪去了？我的钱包呢？"当她办完事回来，它又会惟妙惟肖地学着她的声音说："哟，外面好冷啊。"

凯西不喜欢被关在笼子里，因此帕特经常让它在家中四处游荡。"有了它，可真有趣儿，"她对安妮说，"这使整个家的感觉好多了。"

"我想你也会慢慢感觉好起来的，"安妮说。

"是的，它一天让我大笑四五次呢——人们说大笑对人有益。"

Once a plumber came to repair a leak under the kitchen sink. In the den, Casey cracked seeds in his cage and eyed the plumber through the open door. Suddenly the parrot broke the silence, reciting, "One potato, two potato, three potato, four…"

"What?" asked the plumber.

"Don't poo on the rug," Casey ordered, in Pat's voice.

The plumber pushed himself out from under the sink and marched to the living room. "If you're going to play games, lady, you can just get yourself another plumber." Pat looked at him blankly.

The plumber hesitated. "That was you, wasn't it?"

Pat smiled. "What was me?"

"One potato, two potato—and don't poo on the rug."

"Oh, dear," said Pat. "Let me introduce you to Casey."

Casey saw them coming. "What's going on around here?" he said.

At that moment Pat sneezed. Casey immediately mimicked the sneeze, added a couple of Pat's coughs at her allergic worst and finished with Pat's version of "Wow!" The plumber shook his head slowly and crawled back under the sink.

一次，一名管道工来修厨房水槽底下的一个漏洞。在小房间里，凯西在它的笼子里劈劈啪啪地啄着种子，眼睛透过敞开的门望着这位管道工。突然，鹦鹉打破沉默，背诵道："一块土豆，两块土豆，三块土豆，四……"

"什么？"管道工问。

"别在地毯上吐痰，"凯西用帕特的口气命令道。

管道工从水槽底下抽出身，冲向起居室。"太太，你要是玩游戏，最好再换名管道工。"帕特茫然地望着他。

管道工迟疑了一下问："刚才不是你吗？"

帕特面带微笑。"什么是我？"

"一块土豆，两块土豆——别在地毯上吐痰。"

"噢，我的天，"帕特说，"让我给你介绍一下凯西。"

凯西看见他们走过来，便问："发生了什么事？"

就在那时，帕特打了个喷嚏。凯西立即也打了个喷嚏，并加了一两声帕特过敏症最厉害时的咳嗽，然后模仿着帕特的声音以"哎哟"一声收尾。管道工慢慢地摇了摇头，便又爬回到水槽底下去了。

One morning while Pat was reading the paper, the phone rang. She picked it up and got a dial tone. The next morning it rang again, and again she got a dial tone. The third morning she realized what was going on; Casey had learned to mimic the phone faultlessly.

Once, as Pat opened a soda can at the kitchen table, Casey waddled over and snatched at the can. It toppled, sending a cascade[1] of cola onto her lap and the floor. " *#@!"[2] Pat said. Casey eyed her. "Forget you heard that," she ordered. "I didn't say it. I never say it." Casey kept his beak shut.

Later a real-estate agent arrived to go over some business. She and Pat were deep in discussion when Casey screamed from the den, "*#@!"

Both women acted as though they'd heard nothing.

Liking the sibilance[3], Casey tried it again. "*#@!" he said. And again. "*#@!""*#@!""*#@!"

Caught between humiliation and amusement, Pat put her hand on her guest's arm. "Helen, it's sweet of you to pretend, but I know you haven't suddenly gone deaf." They both broke up laughing.

"Oh, you bad bird," Pat scolded after the agent left. "She's going to think I go around all day saying four-letter words."

"What a mess," Casey said.

---

[1] cascade /kæs'keid/ n. 小瀑布；一连串
[2] *#@! 代表一种难听或骂人的话
[3] sibilance /'sibiləns/ n. 咝音

一天早晨,帕特正在看报,电话铃响了。她拿起电话,听到的是拨号音。第二天早上,电话又响了,她听到的又是拨号音。第三天早上,她才意识到发生了什么事情:是凯西已经准确无误地学会了模仿电话铃响的声音。

有一次,帕特在厨桌旁打开一听汽水,凯西摇摆着走过来,一把抓向了那只汽水罐。罐子倒了,将可乐瀑布般洒落到她的腿上和地板上。"该死!"帕特说。凯西眼睛望着她。"把你听到的忘掉,"她命令道,"我可没那样说。我可根本没说。"凯西始终闭着嘴巴。

后来,一位房地产经纪人来谈生意。她和帕特正深入讨论时,凯西突然从小房间里尖叫道:"该死!"

两个女人都装着好像什么也没听见。

凯西喜欢这种齿擦音,又尝试了一遍。"该死!"说过,它又一而再、再而三地说开了,"该死!""该死!""该死!"

帕特又羞又乐,将手搭到客人的胳膊上。"海伦,你假装没听见,真叫人可亲,但我知道你并没有突然变聋。"她们俩突然都放声大笑起来。

"噢,你这坏鸟,"待经纪人走后,帕特责怪道,"她会以为我整天到处都说脏话呢。"

"真糟糕,"凯西说。

"You're darned right," Pat told him.

Casey's favorite perch[1] in the kitchen was the faucet in the sink; his favorite occupation, trying to remove the washer at the end of it. Once, to tease him, Pat sprinkled a handful of water over him. Casey ceased his attack on the washer and swiveled[2] his head to look at her sharply. "What's the matter with you?" he demanded.

If he left the kitchen, Pat heard him say, "Oh, you bad bird!" Casey was either pecking at her dining-room chairs or the wallpaper in the foyer.

"Is it worth it?" her son, Bill, asked, looking at the damaged front hall.

"Give me a choice between a perfect, lonely house and a tacky[3], happy one," said Pat. "And I'll take the tacky one any day."

But Pat did decide to have Casey's sharp claws clipped. To trim them without getting bitten, the vet wrapped Casey tightly in a towel, turned him on his back and handed him to an assistant to hold while he went to work. A helpless Casey looked at Pat and said piteously, "Oh, the poor baby."

Pat often wondered if Casey knew what he was saying. Sometimes the statements were so appropriate she couldn't be sure. Like the time a guest had lingered on and on talking in the doorway and Casey finally called out impatiently, "Night, night."

---

[1] perch /pə:tʃ/　*n.* 栖息地
[2] swivel /ˈswivl/　*vt.* 旋转；转动
[3] tacky /ˈtæki/　*a.* 棘手的

"你说的可真对,"帕特告诉它。

厨房里,凯西最喜欢的栖息地是水槽里的水龙头;为了占地方,它总是竭力将洗涤者挤到水槽尽头。有一次,帕特逗弄它,掬一捧水洒向了它。凯西停下了对这位洗涤者的攻击,将头转过来机警地望向她。"你怎么了?"它问。

如果它离开厨房,帕特就会听到它说:"噢,你这坏鸟!"凯西要么啄她的餐厅椅子,要么就去啄大厅的壁纸。

"这值吗?"她的儿子比尔看着被破坏的前厅问。

"要是让我在一个完美却孤独的家和一个一塌糊涂却充满欢乐的家之间选择,"帕特说,"我肯定会选择后者。"

但帕特还是决定要给凯西尖利的爪做做修剪。为了修剪时不受咬,兽医用一块毛巾将凯西紧紧包住,翻转使之仰躺,将它递给一名助理攥好,然后才开始工作。无助的凯西望着帕特,可怜兮兮地说道:"噢,可怜的小家伙。"

帕特经常怀疑凯西是否知道它所说的是什么意思。因为时常这些话语都那么的恰如其分,她难以把握。比如那次一位客人一直逗留在门廊里说个不停,凯西最后终于不耐烦地大声叫道:"晚安,晚安。"

Yet, whenever Pat wanted to teach him something, Casey could be maddening. Once she carried him to the living room and settled in an easy chair as Casey sidled up her arm and nestled his head against her chest. Pat dusted the tips of her fingers over his velvet-gray feathers and scarlet tail. "I love you," she said. "Can you say, 'I love you, Pat Myers?'"

Casey cocked an eye at her. "I live on Mallard View," he said. "I know where you live, funny bird. Tell me you love me."

"Funny bird."

Another time Pat was trying to teach Casey "Jingle Bell Rock" before her children and grandchildren arrived for Christmas dinner.

"Where's my glasses?"

"Never mind that. Just listen to me sing." But as Pat sang "Jingle bell, jingle bell, jingle bell rock" and danced around the kitchen, Casey simply looked at her.

Finally Pat gave up. And all through Christmas dinner Casey was silent. When it came time for dessert, Pat extinguished the lights and touched a match to the plum pudding. As the brandy blazed up, with impeccable[1] timing Casey burst into "Jingle bell, jingle bell, jingle bell rock!"

---

[1] impeccable /im'pekəbl/ *a.* 无可挑剔的；无错误的

然而，每逢帕特想教凯西一些东西时，它可能就发狂。有一次，她把凯西带到起居室，在一张安乐椅上坐下来。凯西侧身沿着她的胳膊向上走，最后将脑袋靠在她的胸前。帕特用指尖弹去它柔滑的羽毛和猩红色的尾巴上的灰尘。"我爱你，"她说，"你会说：'我爱你，帕特·迈尔斯'吗？"

凯西斜着一只眼睛望着她。"我住在绿鸭景，"它说，"我知道你住在什么地方，有意思的鸟儿。告诉我你爱我。"

"有意思的鸟儿。"

还有一次，帕特在她的儿女们和孙子孙女们来吃圣诞晚餐之前，试图教凯西唱《铃儿响丁当》。

"我的眼镜哪里去了？"

"别管它。请听我唱。"但当帕特唱着"丁丁当，丁丁当，铃儿响丁当"，在厨房里手舞足蹈时，凯西只是看着她。

最后，帕特放弃了。整个圣诞晚餐期间，凯西一直沉默不语。等开始上甜点，帕特将擦着一根火柴向李子布丁点去，当白兰地被烧着时，凯西不失时机地突然唱了起来："丁丁当，丁丁当，铃儿响丁当！"

Pat's health improved so much she decided to go on a three-week vacation. "You'll be all right," she told Casey. "You can stay with Annie and the kids."

The day her mother was due back, Annie returned Casey to the apartment so he'd be there when Pat got home from the airport.

"Hi, Casey!" Pat called as she unlocked the door. There was no answer. "Holy smokes, it's cold out there!" she said. More silence. Pat dropped her coat and hurried into the den. Casey glared at her.

"Hey, aren't you glad to see me?" The bird moved to the far side of the cage. "Come on, don't be angry," Pat said. She opened the door of the cage and held out her hand. Casey dropped to the bottom of the cage and huddled there.

In the morning Pat tried again. Casey refused to speak. Later that day he consented to climb on her wrist and be carried to the living room. When she sat down, he shifted uneasily and seemed about to fly away. "Please, Casey," Pat pleaded. "I know I was away a long time, but you've got to forgive me."

Casey took a few tentative[1] steps up her arm, then moved back to her knee. "Were you afraid I was never going to come back?" she said softly. "I would never do that."

---

[1] tentative /ˈtentətiv/ *a.* 试探性的

帕特的健康大为好转,所以她决定度一次为期三周的假。"你会没事的,"她对凯西说,"你可以跟安妮和那些孩子呆一段时间。"

在帕特就要回来那天,安妮把凯西送回了母亲的公寓,以便母亲从机场回到家时,它在那里。

"嘿,凯西!"帕特打开门喊道。没有回应。"哟,外面可真冷啊!"她又说。还是没有回应。帕特丢下外套,匆匆走进小房间,只见凯西瞪着她。

"嘿,见到我,你不高兴吗?"鸟儿往笼子的里边移去。"好了,别生气了,"帕特说。她打开笼门,伸出手去。凯西躺倒在笼底,蜷缩在那里。

第二天早上,帕特又试了一次。凯西拒绝开口说话。后来那天它同意爬上她的手腕,被带到了起居室。当帕特坐下来时,凯西不安地动来动去,似乎想飞走。"凯西,"帕特恳求道,"我知道我去了好长时间,但你得原谅我。"

凯西在她的胳膊上试探性地走了几步,然后又回到她的膝盖上。"你是害怕我再也不回来了是吗?"她柔声说道,"我决不会那样做的。"

Casey cocked his head and slowly moved up her arm. Pat crooked her elbow, and Casey nestled against her. Pat stroked his head, smoothing his feathers with her forefinger. Finally Casey spoke. "I love you, Pat Myers," he said.

　　凯西歪着脑袋,慢慢沿着她的胳膊移动。帕特弯起胳膊肘,凯西依偎着她。帕特抚摸着它的脑袋,用食指梳拢它的羽毛。最后,凯西终于开口说道:"帕特·迈尔斯,我爱你。"

The Hunter and a Red Fox

Sly Boy is an American red fox, with a thick coat[1] of light brown fur.

For years, Sly Boy has been stealing chickens and ducks from farms in Virginia. He kills many wild animals, too. Rabbits are one of his favorite foods.

Hunters keep trying to catch Sly Boy. Farmers would like to get rid of him. But Sly Boy is too smart to be caught.

Why has Sly Boy lived so long? One reason is that he is a fast runner. He can run faster than most dogs. His legs, like those of a racehorse, are long for his body.

Once, when Sly Boy was being hunted, dogs chased him for four days. The dogs were worn out. They became so thin they looked like skin and bones.

But not Sly Boy! He ran far ahead of the dogs. Then he stopped to eat berries[2] or a mouse. He even took short naps. As soon as the dogs came close, he ran ahead again.

But sometimes Sly Boy can't run away from the dogs. Then he tricks[3] them. The dogs know many of his tricks. But Sly Boy can always think up a new one!

---

[1] coat *n.* （动物的）皮毛
[2] berry / 'beri/ *n.* 浆果
[3] trick /trik/ *vt.* 哄骗

猎人与红狐

鬼小子是一只美国红狐,身上有层厚厚的浅棕色的皮毛。

几年来,鬼小子一直从弗吉尼亚州的农场偷鸡鸭。它还咬死了好多野生动物。野兔是它最喜欢的美食之一。

猎人们一直想设法猎捕鬼小子。农民们总想摆脱它。但鬼小子聪明伶俐,人们总也逮不住它。

鬼小子为什么会生活这么长时间呢?其中一个原因就是它跑得非常快。它比大多数的狗跑得都快。它的腿就像赛马的腿,跟它的身体一样长。

有一次,猎捕鬼小子时,好多条狗追了它整整四天。那些狗筋疲力尽,看上去都瘦成了皮包骨头。

但鬼小子不是这样!它远远地跑在了那些狗的前面,随后停下来吃浆果或者老鼠。它甚至还睡了短短的午觉。等那些狗一靠近,它就又跑到了前面。

但有时,鬼小子却无法从那些狗身边跑掉。于是,它就玩花招哄骗它们。那些狗知道它的好多花招。而鬼小子总是能想出一个新招!

One day when Sly Boy was being chased, he jumped up onto a fence on the ground. But at last they found it on the fence.

Sly Boy ran on and on. The dogs followed him to a creek. They crossed the creek and sniffed[1]. Sly Boy had not come across. Where had he gone?

Mr. Cook, the hunter, knew that Sly Boy might run in water along the creek. In that way he would fool the dogs. They couldn't smell his scent in the water. But sly Boy had to come out somewhere. Then the dogs could pick up[2] his trail on the sand.

Mr. Cook sent half the dogs upstream and half downstream. The dogs sniffed and sniffed along the creek banks. But they couldn't find Sly Boy's scent.

At last the evening came. When it grew dark, Mr. Cook gave up the hunt and took his dogs home.

Where was Sly Boy all this time? He had gone back to Mr. Cook's farm and eaten a chicken dinner. He was fast asleep in the chicken house when the hunter got home!

By the light of the moon, Mr. Cook saw Sly Boy run off to the woods. "Now, how did he get here?" Mr. Cook wondered. With his dogs, he followed Sly Boy's trail back to the creek. There, under the creek bank, Sly Boy's tracks[3] ended.

---

[1] sniff /snif/ vi. （吸着气）嗅；闻
[2] pick up 找到（被追捕者的踪迹等）
[3] track /træk/ n. 足迹；踪迹

有一天，当鬼小子被追猎时，它纵身一跃跳到了一个篱笆上。但最后，那些狗还是在篱笆上找到了它。

鬼小子跑啊跑。那些狗将它追到了一条小溪边。它们穿过那条小溪，一路嗅着。鬼小子没有穿过去。它到哪里去了呢？

猎人库克先生知道鬼小子可能是沿着小溪跑进了水里。它总是那样捉弄那些狗。它们无法在水里嗅出它的气味。不过，鬼小子不得不出来，走到某个地方。随后，那些狗可能会在沙地上找到它的踪迹。

库克先生将那些狗兵分两路，一路派往上游，另一路派向下游。那些狗沿着小溪岸一路嗅啊嗅，但就是嗅不到鬼小子的气味。

最后，夜幕降临。天越来越黑，库克先生放弃猎捕，带着他的那些狗打道回府。

这段时间，鬼小子一直在哪里呢？他已经回到了库克先生的农场，吃了一顿鸡餐。当猎人回家时，他竟在鸡窝里熟睡呢！

借着月光，库克先生看到鬼小子跑进了树林里。"嗳，它是怎么到这里的呢？"库克先生感到纳闷。他带着那些狗，跟踪鬼小子的踪迹又追回到了小溪边。追到了那里的溪岸下面，鬼小子的踪迹戛然而止。

Sly Boy had hidden under the bank! Right over his head, the dogs had jumped into the water. When they were gone, Sly Boy had run back the way he had come. He had gone right to Mr. Cook's farm.

One day Sly Boy made a mistake. He let the dogs corner[1] him against a cliff. Sly Boy couldn't climb up the cliff. He couldn't go right or left. In front of him were the dogs, coming closer and closer. And Farmer Adams rode right behind them.

It looked like the end for Sly Boy! Mr. Adams pointed[2] his gun.

But suddenly Sly Boy did a surprising thing. He walked straight toward the farmer, looking him right in the eye.

Mr. Adams could have shot Sly Boy easily. But he didn't.

"How can I shoot an animal that looks me in the eye?" he thought. "I can't!"

Mr. Adams just watched as the small animal ran off into the woods.

So Sly Boy, the fox, lives on!

---

[1] corner /'kɔːnə(r)/ *vt.* 将…逼入困境；使走投无路
[2] point *vt.* 把（枪等）对准

鬼小子曾藏在溪岸下面！那些狗刚好从它的头顶跳进了水里。待它们走后，鬼小子又原路返回，跑到了库克先生的农场。

有一天，鬼小子犯了一个错误。它让那些狗逼到了一个悬崖上。鬼小子爬不上悬崖。它既无法向左也无法向右。它面前的那些狗正在越逼越近。而且农民亚当斯骑马就站在它们的背后。

看上去像是鬼小子的末日到了！亚当斯先生将枪瞄准了它。

但鬼小子却突然做了一件令人吃惊的事情。它径直走向了那个农民，直视着那个人的眼睛。

亚当斯先生本可以轻而易举地开枪打死鬼小子。但他没有那样做。

"我怎么能开枪打死一个直视着我眼睛的动物呢？"他想，"我不能！"

亚当斯先生只是望着那只小动物跑进入了树林里。

所以，鬼小子——也就是那只狐狸——一直活在世上！

Fallen in the Mine

Twenty-one-year-old Steve Ridpath stood in front of the entrance to the Charm Mine. He shook with excitement. "By the time we leave here," he said, laughing, "we'll be millionaires!"

Steve was leading a small expedition into an abandoned mine near Paradise Pines, Calif. With him were his 19-year-old brother, Allen, and a fishing buddy, 32-year-old Bobby Erler.

The mine opened at the bottom of a steep, half-mile-wide canyon[1] filled with thick brush and pine trees. It had taken the three men nearly an hour to push through mile of dense vegetation[2] to get to the mine. Now it was almost 11 a.m. that Tuesday, January 25, 1994.

Almost every weekend since grade school, Steve and Allen had scavenged[3] old gold mines in Northern California. Considering themselves experts on old shafts, they would chip off an ounce or two of ore, have it assayed[4] and melted down, then give the bits of gold to their mother, Cathy. Erler had joined them that day to see what the brothers found so fascinating.

---

[1] canyon / ˈkænjən/ n. （通常谷底有溪涧流过的）峡谷
[2] vegetation /vedʒɪˈteɪʃ(ə)n/ n. 植被
[3] scavenge /ˈskævindʒ/ vt. 在…中搜寻有用之物
[4] assay / əˈseɪ/ vt. 经检验证明内含成分

坠入矿井

21岁的史蒂夫·里德帕思站在查姆矿的入口前。他因兴奋而颤抖。"到我们离开这里时,"他笑着说,"我们就要成为百万富翁了!"

史蒂夫领着一小队探险人马进入了加州天堂松附近的一个废矿。同他在一起的是他19岁的弟弟艾伦和32岁的垂钓好友鲍比·厄勒。

那个矿开在一个陡峭的、有半英里宽的、长满浓密灌木丛和松树的峡谷底。三人用了将近一小时,才穿过浓密的丛林到达那个矿。现在已经快到中午11点了。那天是1994年1月25日星期二。

自从上小学以来,几乎每到周末,史蒂夫和艾伦就到加州北部的旧金矿觅宝。他们把自己看成旧矿井专家,凿下一两盎司的矿石,经过检验和冶炼,然后将碎金送给他们的母亲凯西。厄勒那天加入了他们的队伍,想看看兄弟俩的发现到底有多么吸引人。

Clutching his flashlight, Steve climbed over the slippery entrance to the mine and led the way in. The three walked through the long, narrow tunnel, which stretched a quarter-mile into the mountains. Water flowed ankle-deep around their boots.

At the end of the tunnel, Steve held up his hand. "Watch out," he said, shining his flashlight at a ten-by-12-foot hole in the floor. "There's a deep shaft here to drain out water."

Soon the tunnel widened into a three-story-high cavern, where much of the digging had been done. "Hey, I found a seam[1]!" Steve called out, shining his flashlight along a streak of ore on the back wall. Allen sighed. He and his brother had similar interests, but Allen didn't have Steve's nose for gold or his irrepressible energy.

After a couple of hours of exploring, Steve had found several ounces of ore. Allen and Bobby had managed to dig up only a few pieces of quartz. About 2 p.m. Steve's flashlight died. "Let's get going!" he called out.

"Okay," Allen agreed as he continued to search the walls for gold.

Steve pulled the stub of a candle from his pocket, lit it with a cigarette lighter and headed toward the tunnel. Momentarily distracted and eager to get out, he forgot the hole in the floor.

---

[1] seam *n.* 缝；缝口

史蒂夫紧紧地握住手电筒，爬过滑溜溜的矿井入口，领头进去。三人穿过长长的、窄窄的石巷，那条巷道向山里延伸了 1/4 英里。水在他们的靴子四周流动，漫到了脚踝。

到了石巷尽头，史蒂夫举起手。"大家注意，"他说着，将手电筒照在地面上一个 10×12 英尺大小的洞上。"这里有一个深矿井，可以把水抽出来。"

石巷很快就变宽了，成了三层楼高的深洞，那里已经被挖过好多次了。"嘿，我发现一条裂缝！"史蒂夫将手电筒沿着后墙的一条狭长的矿石带照着大声叫道。艾伦叹了口气。尽管他和哥哥有相似的兴趣，但艾伦没有史蒂夫对金子那样的嗅觉，也没有他那样无法抑制的精力。

探索了两三个小时后，史蒂夫已经发现了好几盎司的矿石。艾伦和鲍比想方设法才挖了几块石英矿。大约下午 2 点，史蒂夫的手电筒没电了。"我们往回走吧！"他大声说道。

"好，"艾伦一边继续在石壁上搜寻着金子，一边同意说。

史蒂夫从口袋里掏出一小截蜡烛，用打火机点燃，向石巷里走去。一时间，他的注意力分散了，同时又急于出去，就忘记了地上的那个洞。

Suddenly he felt the dirt give way under him. The drainage shaft! His fingers clawed helplessly at the wet dirt as he fell. He plunged into darkness, his body smashing against the jagged walls of the shaft.

Twenty feet away, Allen heard a loud cry, followed by thumps that ricocheted through the cavern. He whipped around and saw Bobby gaping at the hole in the ground. "He's gone," Bobby said.

Allen threw himself down at the edge of the shaft. "Steeeeve!" he screamed. "Steeeeve!" The only other sound was water running along the mine floor and emptying into the shaft. He shined his flashlight into the hole and saw what appeared to be water below.

Allen teetered[1] desperately over the shaft. He spotted an old drainage pipe, about six inches across, that dropped down one side. "I'm climbing down," he told Bobby.

"You'll get killed," Bobby said. "No telling how deep it is."

"If Steve's alive, he's hurt real bad," Allen said. "I have to do something."

Allen threw off his jacket. Now he wore only a sleeveless T-shirt, cutoff jeans, long-john leggings and boots. The mine was so cold he could almost see his breath.

With his flashlight under his armpit, Allen slid rapidly down the pipe. "I'm coming, Steve!" he yelled several times. No answer.

---

[1] teeter /'ti:tə/ vi. 摇晃

他突然感到脚下的土开始松动。抽水井!他掉下去时,手指无助地抓着那些湿土。他掉进了黑暗中,身体撞在矿井凹凸不平的井壁上。

艾伦在距离20英尺远的地方听到一声大叫,紧接着是咕咚掉进洞里的声音。他飞转过身,看到鲍比对着地上的洞目瞪口呆。"他不见了,"鲍比说。

艾伦扑倒在矿井边。"史——蒂——夫!"他尖声叫道,"史——蒂——夫!"惟一的声音是沿着矿地流淌并落入矿井的声音。他将手电筒照进洞里,看到下面好像是水。

绝望中,艾伦摇晃着趴在矿井边。他看到一根旧排水管,直径大约有6英寸,沿着井壁下行。"我要爬下去,"他对鲍比说。

"你会被淹死的,"鲍比说,"谁也说不准井有多深。"

"如果史蒂夫还活着,他一定会伤得很厉害,"艾伦说,"我必须做点什么。"

艾伦脱掉夹克衫。现在他只穿一件无袖T恤衫、毛边牛仔裤和靴子,绑着长长的裹腿。矿里太冷,他几乎可以看到自己呼出的气。

艾伦腋下夹着手电筒,快速顺着管道滑下去。"我来了,史蒂夫!"他大叫了好几次。但没人回应。

The pipe shuddered as he slipped down it, burning his palms and forearms. The flashlight fell from under his arm. Finally, he heard a faint splash.

As Allen slid toward the bottom of the mineshaft, he saw Steve floating face down in the water, slapping his outstretched arms weakly against the surface. Allen let go and splashed into the cold water.

He slipped his arms around Steve and flipped him on his back. Steve spit up water and started to moan. The water was bitter cold, and Allen's limbs felt numb. I've got to get us out of this water or we'll freeze, he thought.

He saw the drainage pipe continuing into the water. Extending about an inch and a half from the side of the pipe was a joint, just above the water. Holding Steve, Allen dog-paddled over to the pipe, found a toehold in the rock wall and pulled himself up onto the pipe joint. He wedged himself between the pipe and the wall, grabbed hold of Steve's belt and, with all his strength, tried to hoist his 155-pound brother onto his lap. The belt broke, and Steve cried out in pain. Allen grasped him under the arms and pulled him up. The pipe creaked under their weight.

Allen squatted on the joint, balancing on the balls of his feet with Steve's torso in his lap. The air smelled sour and was hard to breathe.

他向下滑时,管道簌簌抖动,他的手掌和前臂被磨得发烫。手电筒从他的腋下滑落下来。最后,他听到了微弱的溅水声。

艾伦滑向矿井底时,看到史蒂夫面朝下浮在水上,有气无力地伸出胳膊拍打着水面。艾伦松开手,扑进了寒冷的水里。

他用双臂抱住史蒂夫的身子,让他仰躺过来。史蒂夫把水吐了出来,开始呻吟。水冰冰冷冷的,艾伦感到四肢麻木。他想,必须从这水里出去,否则会冻僵的。

他看到那个排水管继续向水里延伸。水面上方,管道恰好有一接合处,由管壁向外突出约一英寸半。艾伦抱着史蒂夫用狗爬式游到了管道边,在岩壁上找到了一个小小的支点,将自己拉到了管道接合处上。他将自己揳入管道和岩壁之间,抓住史蒂夫的腰带,然后竭尽全力想要将155磅重的哥哥提到自己的膝盖上。但腰带断裂,史蒂夫痛得大声叫喊。艾伦又抓住哥哥的腋下,将他拉上来。管道在他们的重压下发出嘎吱嘎吱的声音。

艾伦蹲在接合处,将史蒂夫的身体放在膝上,两只前脚掌尽力保持着平衡。空气闻起来酸溜溜的,让人难以呼吸。

From the top of the shaft, Bobby lowered Allen his flashlight with some nylon rope that he had found in the mine. Moments later, Bobby went for help.

Allen ran the flashlight along Steve's body to check for injuries. He saw that his face was badly scraped, and blood was seeping from around his right eye.

Outside the mine, Bobby Erler clawed his way up toward the dirt road. The mile-long climb was exhausting, and he wasn't even sure he was going in the right direction. All the pine trees and scrub bushes looked alike.

Soon Steve opened his eyes halfway. "Where's Mom?" he mumbled.

"You fell down a shaft in the mine," Allen said.

As Steve tried to move, pain shot through his pelvis and rib cage. "Can we climb out?" he asked.

"The pipe would never support us," Allen said.

"I'm gonna[1] die, right?"

"No way," Allen said. "Bobby's going for help."

"Bobby? What if he doesn't remember where this place is? There are hundreds of abandoned mines around here." He shuddered from the pain. "Feels like we're in hell."

---

[1] gonna / ˈgɔnə / （美口）=going to

鲍比从矿井顶端用他在矿里发现的一些尼龙绳将手电筒给艾伦传下来。过了一会儿，鲍比跑去求救。

艾伦将手电筒照在史蒂夫的身上查看伤口。他看到史蒂夫的脸被严重刮伤，血从他的右眼眶四周流了出来。

在矿外面，鲍比·厄勒向上朝那条土路爬去。一英里长的爬行使他筋疲力尽，而且他也拿不准自己爬的方向对不对，所有的松树和灌木丛看上去都很相似。

不久，史蒂夫半睁开了眼睛。"妈妈在哪里？"他咕哝道。

"你掉进矿井里了，"艾伦说。

当史蒂夫尽力想动弹时，他感到骨盆和胸腔一阵剧痛。"我们能爬出来吗？"他问。

"管道是绝对承受不住我们的重量的，"艾伦说。

"我会死，对吗？"

"不会，"艾伦说，"鲍比去求救了。"

"鲍比？他要是不记得这个地方在哪里，怎么办？这附近有几百个废矿。"他因痛苦而剧烈颤抖。"感觉我们就像在地狱中。"

"Too cold for hell," Allen said, trying to smile. Feeling his brother drifting off to sleep, Allen shook him awake.

At 3:20 p.m., Bobby staggered through the door of the Butte County Fire Station, a mile and a half from the top of the canyon. "My friends. Trapped in the Charm Mine," he gasped. "You got to hurry!"

Ten minutes later, Engine 33 arrived at the edge of the canyon but could not maneuver its rescue equipment through the thick brush to the mine. At 4:20, additional firefighters came and started hacking[1] a winding trail down the canyon.

Meanwhile, Cathy, Steve's and Allen's mother—receiving a call from the sheriff's office—rushed to the top of the canyon.

It took firefighters nearly an hour to reach the mine's entrance. But soon after they went in, they turned back. "There may be pockets of explosive gas," one fireman told Cathy on the rim of the canyon. "We need an expert on these old mines."

One hundred miles away, in Susanville, Bob Trussell's phone rang at 5 p.m. Commander of the Lassen County Search and Rescue Team, Trussell, had the only outfit in Northern California trained to lead mine rescues. "I'll pull together my team," he said, "but it'll take some time to get there."

---

[1] hack *vt.* 砍；劈

"相对于地狱来说,这里太冷了,"艾伦尽力笑着说。艾伦感到哥哥昏昏欲睡,就将他摇醒。

下午 3 点 20 分,鲍比跌跌撞撞地进了距离峡谷顶有一英里半的比尤特县消防站的门。"我的朋友们被困在了查姆矿里,"他气喘吁吁地说,"你们得赶快去!"

10 分钟后,33 号消防车赶到了峡谷边,但无法使救援设备穿过浓密的灌木丛到达那个矿。4 点 20 分,又一批消防队员也赶到了,开始砍出了一条下到峡谷的蜿蜒小路。

与此同时,史蒂夫和艾伦的母亲凯西——接到了县治安官办公室的电话——火速赶到了峡谷顶。

消防队员用了将近一小时才到达矿井入口处。但他们进去一会儿后,又折了回来。"也许好几处矿穴中有易爆气体,"其中一名消防队员在峡谷边上对凯西说,"我们需要一名对这些旧矿熟悉的专家。"

下午 5 点,在距离 100 英里远的苏珊维尔,鲍勃·特拉塞尔的电话铃响了起来。作为拉森县搜寻救援队长,特拉塞尔拥有加州北部惟一经过训练的引导矿井救援的人马。"我马上集合队伍,"他说,"但需要一些时间才能赶到那里。"

An hour later, he was leading a convoy of six trucks toward Paradise Pines. Privately, he didn't think the Ridpath boys had much of a chance. In the past year, he'd been called to a dozen cave and mine rescues. A quarter of the victims were dead by the time he reached them. The ones he saved hadn't been down nearly as long as this.

Steve was moaning and drifting in and out of consciousness. Allen wondered how much longer he could hold on to his brother. Allen's arms were aching, and his thighs were numb from squatting. Still, he was determined to keep his arms wrapped around Steve.

Soon the light from the flashlight went out. "We're gonna die, little bro'[1] ," Steve said, moaning.

"No, we're not," Allen argued. A few minutes later, he said, "It feels strange to be taking care of you. You were always saving me."

Steve grimaced[2], made a fist and punched Allen's arm weakly. "Why did you have to come down here?" he asked. "You could have saved yourself."

"You were always protecting me," Allen said. "You were never scared of anything."

"I was scared all the time," Steve said. "I just couldn't let you see it." Steve became quiet, and Allen could feel his brother's breathing slow down.

---

[1] bro'是 brother(s)的缩写
[2] grimace /ɡri'meis/ vi. 作鬼脸

一小时后,他领着由六辆卡车组成的车队向天堂松驶去。他个人认为里德帕思兄弟没多少希望。在过去的一年中,他曾被叫到十几个洞穴和矿里救援。当他们赶到那里时,有1/4的受害者都已经死了。他所救的那些人几乎没有在下面呆这么久的。

史蒂夫呻吟着,昏过去又醒过来。艾伦不知道自己还能抱哥哥多少时间。艾伦的两条胳膊越来越疼,大腿也已蹲得麻木了。然而,他下定决心紧紧地抱住史蒂夫。

手电筒很快就没电了。"我们会死的,弟弟,"史蒂夫呻吟着说。

"不,我们不会的,"艾伦争辩说。几分钟后,他说:"你是对我关照你感到不自在吧。过去你总是救我。"

史蒂夫做了个鬼脸,握拳有气无力地捶了一下艾伦的胳膊。"你为什么要下来呢?"他问,"你本来可以保住自己的。"

"你过去总是保护我,"艾伦说,"你过去从来没怕过什么。"

"我过去一直都很害怕,"史蒂夫说,"我只是不让你看到罢了。"史蒂夫渐渐安静了下来,艾伦感到哥哥的呼吸慢了下来。

"Two young men have been trapped for nearly eight hours," Trussell told the 20-man crew outside the mine. "If they're still alive, they're suffering from hypothermia[1], shock and possibly internal injuries. The mine may be unstable. Now, let's move."

As Allen prayed silently, Steve again fell unconscious. Allen wondered how long they could last. Suddenly he saw something flicker above them. It was a white light!

The light grew stronger and stronger, and then a voice echoed, "Boys? Can you hear me?"

Allen called out, "We're alive!"

Bob Trussell quickly dropped Allen a rope so he could secure Steve to the pipe. Soon the light, radiating from Trussell's helmet, filled the entire shaft. Trussell was being lowered down the center of the shaft by his team. He was surprised at how deep the shaft was—nearly 150 feet.

Dangling in the air a few feet above the water, Trussell tried to wrap a harness around Allen. "What are you doing?" Allen asked, holding on to Steve.

"We're sending you up first," Trussell said.

"I'm not going without Steve."

Around them, the old walls had deep cracks. They could collapse any moment, Trussell thought. "If you want to save your brother's life, you've got to let him go," Trussell said.

---

[1] hypothermia /ˌhaipəuˈθəːmiə/ *n.* 低体温

"两个年轻人被困已经将近 8 小时了,"特拉塞尔在矿外对 20 名队员说,"他们要是还活着,会受着低体温、休克和可能性内伤的煎熬。这个矿可能不稳定。现在,让我们行动吧。"

当艾伦默默祈祷时,史蒂夫又昏迷了过去。艾伦不知道他们还能坚持多久。突然,他看到在他们上方有什么东西闪了一下。那是一道白光!

那道光越来越强,随后回响起一个声音:"孩子们,你们能听到我说话吗?"

艾伦大声喊道:"我们还活着!"

鲍勃·特拉塞尔马上给艾伦放下一条绳子,这样他可以将史蒂夫固定在管道上。不久,那道从特拉塞尔头盔上发出的光顿时充满了整个矿井。特拉塞尔由他的队员们从矿井中央往下放。矿井这么深——将近 150 英尺,这让他感到很吃惊。

特拉塞尔悬在水上方几英尺的空中,试图将安全带裹住艾伦。"你在做什么?"艾伦抱住史蒂夫问。

"我们要先送你上去,"特拉塞尔说。

"没有史蒂夫,我不走。"

他们四周那些旧井壁都有深深的裂缝,随时都可能会坍塌,特拉塞尔想。"要想救你哥哥的命,你就必须松开他,"特拉塞尔说。

Allen finally agreed, and soon felt himself being slowly hauled upward.

Trussell turned to Steve, who was still unconscious. He awoke briefly, and Trussell saw the near death look in his eyes. It took Trussell 30 minutes to strap Steve into a rescue harness clipped on safety rope.

Soon Steve felt himself floating upward. At the top, paramedics stripped off his soaking clothes and started an I.V.

"They're out. They're stable," came word over a walkie-talkie. It was 2 a.m. Wednesday, but dozens of Paradise Pines residents were standing at the lip of the canyon. Cathy cried out with joy.

The two brothers were rushed by ambulance to a nearby hospital. When Steve woke up in the recovery room, Allen was at his side.

"Tell me one thing, bro'," Steve said. "How long would you have stayed down there with me if help hadn't come?"

"If no one had come," Allen said, "I'd still be down there holding you."

艾伦最后表示同意，随后马上就感到自己被慢慢地拉了上去。

特拉塞尔转向史蒂夫，史蒂夫仍昏迷不醒。就在他短暂地醒了一会儿时，特拉塞尔看到了史蒂夫的眼神中濒死的神情。特拉塞尔用了30分钟才给史蒂夫套上绑在安全绳上的救援安全带。

史蒂夫很快感到自己向上浮去。到了顶部，医务人员脱下他湿淋淋的衣服，开始静脉滴注。

"他们出来了，情况很稳定，"步话机传来一个声音。尽管现在已是星期三凌晨两点，但天堂松的几十名居民仍站在峡谷边。凯西因高兴而失声哭了起来。

兄弟俩被救护车火速送到了附近的一家医院。当史蒂夫在康复室醒来时，只见艾伦呆在他的身边。

"告诉我一件事，弟弟，"史蒂夫说，"如果救援队不来，你会在下面跟我呆多久？"

"要是没有人来，"艾伦说，"我会抱着你一直呆在下面。"

The Girl Who Loved the Wind

Every year at about this time, when the air turns sharp, I think about my mother. She was always the first to point out the sign of autumn: the evening sky marbled[1] with streaks of smoke; the sudden urgency of the sparrow's song; the pale, thinned-out morning light.

To mother, autumn was a great book that she'd make up a sea of stories. "You must remember," she would say, "that the leaves which die in the fall are born again in the spring."

Balance and counterbalance; harmony and disharmony; lose and renewal. These seemed to be the themes that ran through my mother's stories—and her life.

A memory: when I was seven, on the night of my mother's 40th birthday, she took me outside to stand beneath a moon so bright it lit up every corner of the garden. "Look through these," my mother said, handing me binoculars[2]. "You see that reddish part? That's the Sea of Tranquility[3]. And the blue shadow to the side? That's the Ocean of Storms." Then she said something about how in life it was necessary to learn to navigate[4] both.

---

[1] marble /'mɑːbl/ *vt.* 使具有大理石花纹
[2] binoculars /bɪˈnɔkjuləz/ *n.* 双筒望远镜
[3] tranquility /ˈtræŋkwiliti/ *n.* 宁静；平静
[4] navigate /ˈnævigeit/ *vt.* 导航

爱风的女孩

一到每年天气转凉的时节,我就想起了母亲。母亲对秋天总是洞察幽微:晚空飘起的袅袅青烟;麻雀突如其来的惊叫;淡淡的、稀疏的晨光。

对母亲来说,秋天是一本大书。她常有讲不完的故事。她常说:"你一定要记住,秋天坠落的树叶,春天还会重新萌芽。"

平衡与失衡、和谐与失调、丧失与获得,这些似乎永远是母亲的故事——她生活的主题。

记得我 7 岁那年,在母亲 40 岁生日那天夜里,她带着我走出门外站在月光下,只见皎洁的月光照亮了花园的每个角落。"你拿住这个看看,"母亲将望远镜递给我说,"你看到那淡红色的部分了吗?那是宁静之海。你看到那蓝色的阴影了吗?那是风暴之洋。"之后,她又说,生活之中既有宁静也有风暴,有必要学会在两者之间航行。

To be honest, I didn't see either the Sea or the Ocean. Staring through the binoculars at the moon, I saw only my mother's face swimming about me through pale stars in a dark blue sky.

I thought about this in the cool, hickory[1]-scented evening air of my own garden. I watched the moon appear and disappear as it worked its way through the delicate tracery[2] of trees outlined on the horizon.

Before I knew it, I was zipping[3] into the past.

My mother loved the wind. And she would often recite this poem to me:

Who has seen the wind?
Neither you nor I,
But when the trees bow down their heads,
The wind is passing by.

She told me once about how when she was a little girl walking to church, the wind lifted her hat off her head and carried it to the bottom of a steep hill. It was her best hat, navy straw, and she was afraid she'd be scolded for losing it. So she climbed down through the underbrush. She retrieved[4] the hat—along with an abandoned kitten that was to become her most beloved pet. She named Zephyr[5], she told me, because he was as light as a gentle breeze.

---

[1] hickory /ˈhikəri/ n. 山核桃
[2] tracery /ˈtreisəri/ n. 窗花格
[3] zip vi. 有力而快速地移动
[4] retrieve /riˈtriːv/ vt. 取回
[5] Zephyr /ˈzefə/ n. 西风之神

说真心话，我既没看到什么宁静之海，也没看到风暴之洋。我仅仅是透过望远镜望着月亮。在深蓝色的、淡淡的星空下，我仅仅看到母亲的脸在我的眼前晃来晃去。

我站在凉风习习、弥漫着山胡桃气息的花园中回想着这幕情景。只见月亮穿过远处地平线上精美的窗格一样的树林，时隐时现。

我的思绪飞扬，又回到了从前。

母亲爱风，她常常给我吟诵：
谁看到过风？
你没看到，我也没看到。
但当树枝晃动时，
风正在徐徐吹过。

有一次，她告诉我说，小时候她上教堂时，风掀掉了她的帽子，刮到了一个陡峭的山坡下面。那是她最漂亮的帽子——一顶深蓝色的草帽。她害怕自己回家挨骂，就爬下山穿过灌木丛，找到了草帽，还带回了一只被人遗弃的小猫。后来，这只小猫成了她最心爱的宠物。她给它起名叫"西风之神"，她告诉我说，那只小猫轻飘飘，如柔风一般。

There's an old photograph of them in the family album. My mother, about ten years old, is holding the small gray cat which is struggling to jump out of her arms. The wind is blowing a few loose strands of her long, dark hair across her eyes. This girl who loved the wind is smiling—perhaps at the feel of the breeze touching her face.

My mother told me that as a child she loved dogs but was not allowed to have one. So she invented a spotted, medium-size blood-hound named Morley. Every night before going to bed she would go to the back door and call him in.

Usually, at this point, my mother would begin acting out the story. I can picture it even now: my mother in a long nightgown, her black braid falling to her waist, standing at the door on a frosty night, called, "Morley, Morley. Here, Morley."

Finally, as I smiled at the child my mother was, I could think of her without deep feelings of sadness and loss. I could picture her, to the sound of bagpipe[1], practicing the Highland fling[2] in front of a mirror.

And so I sat the other night on the floor of my room holding my mother's handbag. I had brought it home with me from the hospital on the day of her death, but had not been able to open it.

---

[1] bagpipe /'bægpaip/ *n.* 风笛
[2] Highland fling 轻快的苏格兰高地舞

家里的相册中有一张她和小猫在一起的旧照片。当时，母亲才 10 岁左右。只见她搂着那只小灰猫，小猫却挣扎着想跳出她的怀抱。她的乌黑的长发随风拂动，飘洒在她的眼睛上面。这个爱风的女孩微微含笑——也许是感到轻风拂面，她才那样笑的吧。

母亲还对我说，小时候她很爱狗，但家里人不准她养。她日思夜想，好像真的养了一只中等个头的花警犬，她还给它起名叫"莫利"。每天夜里上床睡觉之前，她都要走到后门口叫它进来。

每当此时，母亲总是活灵活现地向我表演一番。甚至现在我还能想像出当时的情景：只见母亲穿着长长的睡袍，梳着垂至腰间的乌黑辫子，在霜花满地的夜色中站在门口叫道："莫利，莫利，过来，莫利。"

最后，我对着童年时的母亲笑了。我回忆她，但没有深深的悲伤和惆怅。我仿佛看到母亲伴着风笛之声，在镜子前面跳起了热情奔放的苏格兰高地舞。

随后，我坐在自己房间的地板上，抱着母亲的手提包，这是我在母亲去世那天从医院带回家的，但一直没打开。

Inside, along with the lipstick, wallet and photos of her grandchildren, I found a folded piece of paper upon which my mother had written these lines from nature writer Wendel Berry:

"Always in the big woods when you step off alone into a new place there will be, along with curiosity and excitement, a little nagging[1] of dread. It is the ancient fear of the unknown, your first bond with the wilderness you are going into."

Just the sort of thing Mother would say, who could still teach me after all these years.

I went downstairs and opened the kitchen door. And suddenly a breeze blew in. You've been six years out of the wind, I thought. Then I found myself saying, to no one in particular:

Who has seen the wind?
Neither you nor I,
But when the trees bow down their heads,
The wind is passing by.

---

[1] nagging *n.* 唠叨;指责不休

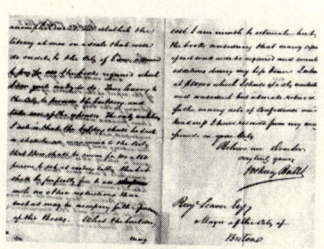

  与唇膏、钱夹和外孙们的照片放在一起的是一张折叠着的纸,上面是她抄录的自然派作家温德尔·贝利的文章片断:

  "一味生活在茫茫丛林,一旦走出来进入一个新天地,你就会有点儿好奇、兴奋,甚至还会有点儿恐惧——这是你对未知世界的古老的恐惧,也就是你和即将进入的荒原的第一次联系。"

  这和母亲所说的话如出一辙。正因为如此,才使我受益了这么多年。

  我走下楼,打开厨房门。一阵轻风翩然入内。你已经与风隔绝了6年了啊,我暗自想道。同时,我发现自己在默默自语:

谁看到过风?
你没看到,我也没看到。
但当树枝晃动时,
风正徐徐吹过。

The Girl out of the Swamp

At first light, when fog was thick on a small lake in the Canadian wilderness, Angela Hanson sat close to her father and listened carefully to him.

"It'll take at least three days, and don't try to do it in less," the man warned. Lying beside the small fire, he groaned as he moved the wrapped leg that was splinted[1] with a tree limb. "A day to get back to Sturgeon Lake—then follow the Maligne River and carry the canoe across both falls."

"Then Minn, McAree, and Crooked Lakes—follow the route I've marked here."

"Don't worry, Dad," Angela told him. "I can do it." But she was worried. They were more than 100 miles from the nearest help. The wilderness she had to cross frightened her.

Angela couldn't believe that such a wonderful adventure could become so frightening. Her father loved canoeing, and they had gone together many times on camping trips along close-to-home rivers. Angela's mother had died three years before.

---

[1] splint *vt.* 用夹板固定；（夹板似地）扶持

闯出沼泽的少女

曙光初现，加拿大荒原的一个小湖上大雾弥漫，安杰拉·汉森紧挨她父亲坐在那里，仔细听他说话。

"那至少要花三天，没有三天别想把它做好，"她父亲警告说。他躺在小火边，一边挪动着那条用一根树干固定着的、包裹着的腿，一边呻吟着。"要返回斯特金湖需要一天——然后顺马林格河而下，而且要扛着独木舟穿过两条瀑布。"

"随后，穿过明湖、迈克里湖和克鲁克特湖——顺着我在这里标出的路线向前走。"

"别担心，爸爸，"安杰拉对他说，"我能行。"但她很担心。距离他们最近的可以求援的地方在100英里以上。她要穿过的茫茫荒原使她非常害怕。

安杰拉无法相信这样妙不可言的奇遇会变得如此让人害怕。她父亲喜欢划独木舟，而且他们一块儿沿着离家不远的那些河野营过很多次。安杰拉的母亲在三年前已经去世。

They had planned for months to take the trip into Canada. Her father had warned, "The land is wild. No one can put up a building there, and you can take only what you can carry on your back. Bush pilots[1] can't even land there, unless they really need to."

When Angela turned twelve, she knew that the canoe trip would be soon. Her birthday gift was a new two-person canoe, smaller and lighter than the one they owned. She was overjoyed—she had wanted one for two years. Thin and strong, she had soon learned how to carry the boat alone—pulling it onto her lap and then standing and flipping[2] it up with one move.

"You'll have to carry with the canoe," her father explained. "If I carry the gear[3], I'll have all I can handle."

They spent many evenings planning the trip, packing their gear, and oiling the canoe. Finally the day came when they were to leave. They left their car at the ranger station[4] and started out on foot.

---

[1] bush pilot 飞行于人烟稀少地区的飞行员；习惯于无地面导航的飞行员
[2] flip vi 扑动
[3] gear /giə(r)/ n. 帆具
[4] ranger /ˈreindʒə/ station 护林站

他们对去加拿大旅行已经计划了好几个月。她父亲曾说过:"那个地方是荒野,没有人能在那里盖起一座大楼,而且你只能把你扛得动的东西背在背上。甚至技术高超的飞行员也无法在那里着陆,除非他们迫不得已。"

安杰拉 12 岁时,知道很快就要进行一次划独木舟旅行了。她的生日礼物就是一艘可以坐两人的新独木舟,与他们原来拥有的那艘比起来又小又轻。她欣喜若狂——两年以来她一直想拥有这样一艘小船。她虽瘦却很结实,马上就学会了怎样独自扛船——将它拉到她的膝间,然后站起来,一下子把它翻到背上。

"你必须得自己带着独木舟,"她父亲解释说,"如果能带着帆具,我就可以应付自如。"

他们花费了许多个夜晚计划这次旅行,打点行囊,给独木舟上油。最后,他们动身的那天到了。他们将汽车留在了护林站,就徒步出发了。

They traveled slowly—a day of canoeing, then a day to rest and explore. They spent two nights at each camp. They worked their way along water that seemed to flow forever, past islands and sandbars[1]. They passed dark-green forests cut apart by swiftly rushing water. Far to the north of Sturgeon Lake, they tracked through a world far away from their home in the city.

They had been out nearly two weeks when it happened. Climbing around a waterfall, Angela's father slipped on a wet stone and fell into the pool below. Angela rushed over to help. But the man's face showed pain. His right leg was broken above the knee. "Cut some limbs for a splint," he said through gritted[2] teeth. He pushed the bone into place himself, almost passing out from the pain. Angela wrapped the leg tightly with torn strips of clothing. When they started back together, they moved too slowly.

At the speed they were going, their food wouldn't last for half the trip ahead. They were off the main traveled routes. There was no hope that other campers might find them.

Finally, they faced the fact that they had only one hope. Angela had to go alone for help.

---

[1] sandbar /'sændbɑː(r)/ n. 河口沙洲
[2] gritted /gritid/ a. 咬紧的

他们走得很慢——划一天独木舟，然后再休息和探索一天。他们在每个营地过两个夜晚。他们沿着源远流长的河水向前走，经过了一座座小岛和一个个沙洲。他们穿过被汹涌澎湃的大河分开的深绿色的森林。在斯特金湖北部的远处，他们穿过了一个远离他们城市之家的世界。

出事那天，他们已经出去将近两周了。安杰拉的父亲爬着绕过一条瀑布时，在一块湿石头上滑了一下，掉进了下面的水潭。安杰拉冲过去想助他一臂之力。但见她父亲的脸上露出了痛苦的神情。他膝盖以上的右腿部分骨折了。"砍些树干支撑一下，"他透过牙缝说着，将骨头推回原位，疼得几乎昏了过去。安杰拉用撕烂的布条紧紧地裹住父亲的那条腿。当他们一起返回时，他们移动得很慢很慢。

按他们走的速度，他们的食物维持前面一半的行程都不够。他们离开了主要的旅行路线。其他野营队员不可能找到他们。

最后，他们面对的只有一个希望，那就是安杰拉不得不独自一人去求助。

She made the best camp she could and gathered a good supply of wood for the fire. She put water on the fire to boil. Then, she took her sleeping bag and some dried meat, put the canoe into the water, and started her journey.

"I can do it!" she said over and over.

By the time the sun was up, she felt more sure of herself. She felt that she had gotten stronger in the past two weeks.

Even so, it was evening before she reached Sturgeon Lake. The wind had made the water rough, and she stopped to rest before going on. Even though she hadn't meant to, she fell asleep. She awoke in darkness. Looking at her watch, she saw that it was past midnight.

She couldn't get back to sleep. She knew she shouldn't travel at night, but as she flashed her light on the map, she could see no chance of a mistake. Still, she could hear her father's voice telling her not to travel at night.

That leg could be a lot worse than Dad lets on[1], she thought. She's got to get to a hospital. I can't waste any time.

She rolled up her sleeping bag, pushed the canoe into the water, and started across Sturgeon Lake.

---

[1] let on 泄密

她尽其所能地搭了一个最好的营地,收集了好多木柴用来生火。她将水放在火上烧,随后带着她的睡袋和一些干肉,将独木舟放进水里,然后开始了她的行程。

"我能行!"她一遍又一遍地说。

到太阳升起时,她对自己更有信心了。她感到自己在过去的两周中变得更加坚强了。

即使这样,还没等她到达斯特金湖,天已黄昏,风起河涌。于是,她停下来歇脚。即使她不想睡,还是倒头睡去。她在黑暗中醒来,看了看手表,发现已过午夜。

她无法再入睡。她知道自己不应该在夜里旅行。她用手电筒照着地图,以确保自己万无一失。她仍然可以听到父亲的声音,告诉她不要在夜间旅行。

那条腿可能会比爸爸流露出的表情要糟得多,她心想。她必须得赶到一家医院。不能浪费一分一秒。

她卷起睡袋,将独木舟推进水里,开始划过斯特金湖。

At first, big waves were frightening in the dark. But she paddled[1] hard and kept the wind in her face. The pitching[2] of the canoe finally slowed down as she came close to the shore.

The moon was breaking through a fast-moving cloud as she worked her way down the still water of a narrowing bay. But she had the feeling that she was forgetting something. And when she suddenly remembered, she felt a chill that didn't come from the night air.

There was fast water ahead on the Maligne River—fast water her father made her promise that she wouldn't try to run during the day, much less at night.

She waited for some time, studying the map by flashlight. But she finally decided to go on. She'd stay close to shore, she promised herself, and head in when she noticed fast water.

The wind was loud in the trees. She knew she wouldn't be able to hear the fast water, and she grew more afraid. After about half an hour, she grounded[3] the canoe and began walking along the shore, using her flashlight as little as possible. Finding nothing, she drifted the canoe down and tried again. On her fourth search of the shore, she was grateful to find the worn path of a trail leading off through the trees.

---

[1] paddle /'pæd(ə)l/ vt. 划动
[2] pitching n. 颠簸
[3] ground vt. 把…放在地上；使搁浅

起先，黑暗中的大浪令人恐惧。但她还是拼命划桨，迎风向前。当她最后靠近岸边时，飞速行进的独木舟慢了下来。

她顺着一个越来越窄的静静的河湾前行，月亮正拱破一块飞速移动的云彩。她觉得自己忘记了什么事。而当她突然想起来时，感到一股飕飕的冷气，但这冷气不是来自夜空。

前面的马林格河有急流——她父亲曾对她说过，那个急流她白天也别想划过去，更不用说是在夜里。

她等了一段时间，借着手电筒查看着地图。但她最后还是决定继续前进。她要贴近岸边，她对自己保证说，然后当她注意到急流时，就向前划去。

风在树林中呼呼作响。她知道自己无法听到急流声，越来越害怕。大约半小时后，她将独木舟固定好，开始沿着河岸走了起来，尽可能少用手电筒。由于没有发现什么东西，她便将独木舟漂下去，又试了一次。经过四次对岸上的搜索，谢天谢地她找到了一条穿过树林的崎岖小路。

She wasn't sleepy, and the trail seemed clear enough to follow by moonlight. I might as well go on, she thought. If I run into rough cover, I'll rest right there until morning.

Shouldering [1] the canoe, her sleeping bag packed on her back, she walked for more than a mile through the dark woods. Then she paddled on, west and a little south, staying close to shore. The wind was dying now, and she wasn't worried about not hearing the second of fast water.

I just have to carry the canoe one more time, and then it will be straight going all the way to the falls above Minn Lake, she thought. I'll bet I gained half a day by going on last night.

She carried the canoe the second time in the early dawn, and she felt much better as the sky grew lighter. Even when the trail seemed longer than it should have, she didn't stop to rest. Just as her legs were about to give out [2], she came to water again. Putting the canoe in, she paddled off. She now let her legs rest while her arms did all the work. She could go only a few yards, so she kept close to shore.

Still, a feeling that something was wrong began to trouble her. Suddenly, she knew that she no longer felt the pull of the water. Drifting slowly, she could see farther and farther, but she saw no sight of the other shore.

---

[1] shoulder *vt.* 用肩扛着
[2] give out 筋疲力尽

她没有睡意。在月光照耀下，小路清晰可辨，她可以顺路而行。我还是继续走吧，她心里想。如果进入汹涌的地段，我就在那里一直呆到明天早上。

她肩上扛着独木舟，背上背着睡袋，走了一英里多穿过黑暗的丛林，随后继续向前划，向西，稍微偏南一点，紧贴着河岸。风现在渐渐息了。她不再为听不到第二次急流声而担心了。

我只是不得不再次扛着独木舟，随后一路走到明湖上方的那些瀑布，她心里想，我敢打赌昨天夜里我走了有半天的路程。

晨曦中，她第二次扛起了独木舟。天空变得越来越亮，她感到好多了。甚至在小路看起来比原来的还要长时，她也没有停下来休息。正当两条腿要筋疲力尽时，她又一次来到水边。她将独木舟放进水里，划了开去。在两臂划动的同时，她就让两腿歇着。她只能走几码远，所以她一直贴着岸边。

然而，一种要出错的感觉开始困扰着她。突然，她发现自己再也感觉不到水的拉力了。慢慢地漂流，她可以看得越来越远了，但她还是看不见对岸。

She looked at the map for a long time before she knew what had happened. The night before, she'd forgotten there was another trail, and she'd taken the wrong one. She wasn't on the Maligne River now. She was far south of the route her father had marked. She was nearing a bottom bay of Wink Lake.

Angela felt sick when she thought about the distance she would have to backtrack[1]. Instead of reaching help in three days, she'd need at least four. The map seemed to stare back at her as she looked at it.

"Wait a minute," she suddenly burst out. Less than four miles to the south lay Darky Lake. Then an easy stretch of paddling would take her into Crooked Lake. Just a small blank space on the map separated her from a shortcut that could correct her mistake.

How bad can four miles be? She asked herself. If it took all day, I'd still be ahead.

She knew her father had told her to stick to the marked route. But now that she'd gotten so far off course, wouldn't her father want her to do what she thought best? The land to the south was flat and low. There couldn't be big trees or cliffs to stop her.

She decided to paddle on to the south.

---

[1] backtrack /'bæktræk/ vt. 由原路返回；追踪

她看了好一会儿地图，随后才明白是怎么回事。前一天夜里，她忘记了还有一条小路，而且她走错了路。她现在不是在马林格河上。她离开了父亲标记的路线的南端，就要靠近文克湖的一个底湾了。

安杰拉想到她不得不向回走的距离就感到恶心。三天内，她找不到救援人员了，至少需要四天。她看着地图，地图似乎也在盯着她。

"等一下，"她突然脱口喊道。南边不到 4 英里处就是黑湖。随后，一阵轻松的划行将她带进了克鲁克特湖。地图上小小的空白处将她和一条可能会纠正她错误的捷径隔离开来。

四英里可能会多糟糕呢？她扪心自问。如果那需要一天时间，那我仍然来得及。

她知道，她父亲曾对她说过要沿着标记过的路线走。但既然已经偏离了这么远，难道她父亲不想让她做她认为最好的事吗？南部的土地低而平坦。不可能有大树或悬崖阻挡她。

她决定继续向南划行。

Reaching the shore, she remembered to fill her water bottle before picking up the canoe. Then she worked her way slowly through the swamp grass, her shoes sticking in the mud at each step. She placed the canoe in the water and tried to paddle.

The water wasn't deep enough. She climbed out to carry the canoe again. It became harder and harder to free her feet.

For hours, she worked on. Sometimes, she could move the canoe only by rocking[1] it and pulling on clumps[2] of grass. Once, when she stepped out to carry the canoe, she felt herself sinking down and down. With a frightened cry, she grabbed the side.

Now, she knew that she was trapped in a world that was neither land nor water. It was quicksand[3] and a waste of rotting plants.

She kicked out at the softness that seemed to be pulling her down, and she soon knew that she was moving the canoe. With her weight out, the light boat was sliding over the surface. She could swim and push the canoe.

Hour after hour, she fought on. Sometimes she found water enough to paddle for a while. At other times, the ground was firm enough for her to carry the canoe. But for the most part, she made greater distance through the swamp softness by kicking and swimming, with one hand on the canoe rim.

---

[1] rock *vt.* 摇动；晃动
[2] clump /klʌmp/ *n.* 一团
[3] quicksand /ˈkwiksænd/ *n.* 流沙

到了岸上,她想起在扛起独木舟之前要把水瓶灌满,随后慢慢地穿过沼泽草地,她每走一步,鞋子就陷进泥里。她将独木舟放进水里,尽力划行。

水不够深。她爬出来,又扛起了独木舟,两只脚越来越难挪动。

她连续走了好几个小时,有时只能通过摇晃和拽一团团的草来移动独木舟。有一次,当她跨步出来去扛独木舟时,发现自己陷得越来越深。随着一个可怕的叫声,她抓住了船边。

如今,她知道自己陷入了既不是水也不是土的境地中。那是流沙和腐烂植物的沼泽。

她飞脚踢出了似乎要把她拽下去的、软软的沼泽;随后,她马上意识到她在移动独木舟。随着身体的挣脱,轻飘飘的小船在表面上滑行起来。她又可以游动向前推动独木舟了。

时间一小时一小时地过去了,她仍在挣扎,有时发现水够深就划上一阵。她不时会碰上硬地,只得扛着独木舟。但多数时间,她都是将一只手放在船沿上,通过踢腾和游动穿过漫长的、软软的沼泽。

Time lost all meanings for her until she saw how low the sun was sinking. Then, the thought of being trapped into the swamp by darkness drove her on, even when she felt she couldn't move another inch or draw another breath.

The light was falling fast. She kept trying, foot by foot. But when it became too dark for her to see, she didn't dare go farther.

It took all her remaining strength to pull her body back into the canoe. She felt sick from the swamp, the smell, from being tired, and from defeat. She put her head on the pack, pulled her jacket over her head to guard against mosquitoes, and dropped to sleep.

She woke with the light, jumping up and staring around her like a wild animal. She waited a moment before she forced herself back into the swamp again.

She'd gone less than 200 yards when she came to water deep enough for paddling. Within half an hour, she was out of t he swamp and had reached Darky Lake.

She heard herself laughing aloud. She swamped and drained the canoe to clean it. Splashing about in the cold, clean water, she washed herself and her clothes at the same time.

时间对她来说已经失去了所有意义，直到她看到太阳渐渐西沉。随后，一想到要被黑暗陷入沼泽之中，她就拼命向前，甚至当她感到寸步难移或无法再喘口气时也没停下来。

白天正在迅速逝去。她一步一步，继续努力着。但当天越来越黑无法看见时，她就不敢再向前走了。

她用尽了剩下的力气将身体移回到了独木舟里。由于沼泽、恶臭、疲惫以及失败，她感到恶心。她将头靠在行李上，把夹克衫拉到头上防止蚊子叮咬，随后倒头睡去。

天亮了，她也醒来了。她一跃而起，像一头野兽那样扫视四周。她在强迫自己回到沼泽中之前，又等了一会儿。

她走了不到 200 码，便来到了河水深得足以划船的地方。不到半个小时，她就走出沼泽地，到达了黑湖。

她听到自己大声笑了起来。她将独木舟弄出来清洗干净。站在寒冷清澈的水中泼着水，她将身体和衣服同时也洗了洗。

All at once, she felt hungry. She ate more than a full day's ration for breakfast. She didn't have to save food now. She was halfway across the lake by the time the sun rose fully. Her clothes were drying fast in the wind. Paddling now seemed easy.

By late morning she was winding[1] her way through the last of the islands in Crooked Lake, and she could see the island where she knew she could find the ranger station.

Less than fifteen minutes after Angela Hanson had told her story, a radio call had gone off[2]. A small plane from Ely touched down on Basswood Lake. Then Angela was in the air, and the ground and water below her seemed too tiny to be real.

Following the map, she tried to spot the swamp through which she had come, but she couldn't be sure she was looking at the right place. Now, it was all spots of green and blue.

"When did you start out?" the pilot asked.

"Day before yesterday morning," Angela answered.

---

[1] wind *vt.* 蜿蜒而行
[2] go off 使发射

突然，她感到饥肠辘辘。她这顿早饭吃的东西比一天的定量还要多。她现在不必节约食物了。到太阳完全升起来时，她距离湖对岸只剩
一半路程了。她的衣服在风中很快就干了。现在划船好像也容易了。

到上午晚些时候，她蜿蜒着穿过克鲁克特湖的最后一个岛。她可以看到那座岛了，知道自己可以在那里找到护林站。

在安杰拉·汉森讲完她的故事后不到 15 分钟，无线电信号就发射了出去。从埃里起飞的一架小飞机在巴斯木湖上低空飞行。随后，安杰拉就到了空中，她下面的地面和河水似乎太小了，显得不那么真实。

顺着地图指的方向，她尽力想通过她来的方向找到那个沼泽，但她拿不准她看的地方是否就是那个地方。现在那里都是蓝蓝绿绿的斑点。

"你是什么时候出发的？"飞行员问。

"前天早上，"安杰拉答道。

The man nodded. "That's about right for that trip. Moving steadily without burning yourself out[1]."

Angela tried to think of an answer and then gave up. She wasn't trying to hide her mistake. It was hard to tell a stranger. Smoke rose from the end of a small lake ahead. The plane began dropping. She could see the camp and then the figure[2] of a man, standing with the aid of a tree limb.

Later, there would be time enough to talk it all out with her dad.

---

[1] burn oneself out 使筋疲力尽
[2] figure /ˈfɪɡə(r)/; (US) ˈfɪɡjər/ n. 人影

飞行员点点头。"就是这段路程。稳住劲儿，别让自己累垮了。"

安杰拉尽力想回答，随后又放弃了。她不是在设法掩饰自己的错误，而是很难告诉一个素不相识的人。烟从前面的一个小湖尽头袅袅升起。飞机开始下降。她可以看到那个营地了，随后看到了一个男人的身影，在一个树干的扶助下站在那里。

之后，她就有足够时间跟爸爸一五一十地说起那件事了。

We'll Remember, Tiger

Gwyn, my youngest daughter, held Tiger as we drove down the country road to the vet's on what was to be his last Friday morning. Privately, both of us nursed a forlorn hope. We joked and laughed, trying to ignore the shadow hanging over the cat sitting very quietly in her arms.

At 16, Tiger was old for a cat. In quiet dignity[1], he let Gwyn pet him, perhaps understanding that this was a special trip. I glanced at the two as I drove, and thought back to the day when Tiger entered our lives.

He had been a Christmas present to my second son. Brian, handed down—as were his clothes and toys—from his older brother. Sadly, even our dogs had neglected[2] Brian, responding much more eagerly to my commands, and those of my wife and older boy.

---

[1] dignity *n.* 尊严；高贵
[2] neglect /niˈglekt/ *vt.* 忽视；疏忽

虎儿在我心

虎儿在世的最后一个星期五的上午,我们驱车沿着一条乡间小路向兽医院行驶。小女儿格温怀抱着虎儿。我们俩都抱着一线渺茫的希望。我们一路说笑,尽力不去想笼罩在猫身上的阴影。此刻,虎儿正静静地躺在格温的手臂上。

虎儿已经 16 岁了。对猫来说,已算年迈。它带着尊严让格温抚摸它,也许懂得这是一次特殊旅行。我一边开车,一边向她们俩瞥视,回想着虎儿进入我们生活的那一天的情景。

虎儿原来是别人送给二儿子布莱恩的圣诞礼物。那时,布莱恩 6 岁,一心想获得一件只属于他一个人的东西,一件不是从他哥哥那里传下来的东西,他的衣服、玩具都是这样来的。不幸的是,甚至连我们家的狗都和布莱恩疏远,总是更乐意听从我、我的妻子和大男孩的命令。

And so, on Christmas Day 1954, I rose early with my wife to put the tiny kitten a neighbor had given us into the stocking that Brian had carefully tacked to the mantel[1] the night before. The first of my vivid memories involving Tiger is the look of joy on Brian's face when he saw the kitten's head poking out of the stocking, and heard the plaintive[2] "meow" that proved his present was alive.

From then on, Tiger's life was filled with love. Brian cared for him tenderly, fed him, played with him. For a sometimes rough, sometimes clumsy child, Brian showed a gentleness with Tiger that was amazing. And late children, I would invariably[3] find Tiger on Brian's bed, stretched out beside him.

My next clear memory of Tiger is also a happy one, which came after near-tragedy. One evening our next-door neighbor rang the front doorbell. "I'm sorry to have to tell you this," she said when my wife answered the door," but when I backed out of the driveway this noon, I'm afraid I ran your cat. I tried to help him, but he jumped up and ran away. I don't know where he went or how badly he was hurt."

---

[1] mantel *n.* 壁炉架
[2] plaintive /ˈpleintiv/ *a.* 悲哀的；哀伤的
[3] invariably /inˈveəriəb(ə)li/ *ad.* 总是

因此，1954年圣诞节那天，我和妻子起得很早，将邻居赠送我们家的小猫放进了布莱恩昨晚细心钉在壁炉架上的长统袜内。我对虎儿最初的鲜明回忆之一是，当布莱恩看到小猫从长统袜里探出脑袋，并听到凄哀的咪咪声，待证明他的礼物是活物而不是玩具时，他一下子绽开了笑容。

从那时起，虎儿的生命中就充满了爱。布莱恩温柔周到地照料和喂养它，跟它玩耍。尽管他是一个时而粗鲁，时而笨拙的孩子，但他对虎儿表现出的温柔简直让人吃惊。深夜，当我检查孩子们入睡情况时，发现虎儿安睡在布莱恩的床上，四肢伸展卧在他的身边。

我能清楚地记得的有关虎儿的另一件事，同样让人高兴。那是在几乎酿成惨祸之后发生的事。一天晚上，一位邻居按响了我家前门的门铃。当我的妻子前去开门时，她说："告诉你一件事，真对不起。今天中午我在车道上倒车出去时，我怕是压着你们家的猫了。我想看看它是否受了伤，但它竟跳起来跑了。我不知道它到哪里去了，也不知道它受伤了没有。"

Four weeks passed with no sign of Tiger. Soldier-like, Brian tried to hide his fear that his friend had crawled away to die. It was a fear we all shared. And we came to accept his death—all of us except Brian.

Every evening Brian would go to the door and call Tigers name. Finally, on the 28th day after the neighbor's announcement, Brian had an answer. Out from under the front porch came Tiger, his tail high, walking with the pride and majesty[1] he customarily displayed, behaving as if he had never been away. As he approached the door, Brian's face was transformed[2] with joy. But neither he nor Tiger displayed open affection in front of the family. There was a calm acceptance, an honoring by each of the other's dignity. That night, though, when I checked Brian's room, I saw that his cheeks were wet and a blissful smile was on his face. And his arm encircled his cat, who lay purring[3] quietly beside him.

The years passed. Now Tiger was 12, Brian 18. And Brian, feeling acutely the communication gap between generations, suffered an identity crisis. The tensions were too great. He had to getaway. And so he left his home to join others of his generation who were seeking answers to questions for which their parents had no answers, in part because they did not know what the questions were.

---

[1] majesty /ˈmædʒisti/   n. 威严；雄伟
[2] transform /trænsˈfɔːm/   vt. 转换；改造
[3] purr   vi. 发出呜呜声

四个星期过去了,虎儿一直没有露面。像勇敢的军人那样,布莱恩虽然担心他的朋友可能已经爬到人们找不到的地方死去了,却将忧虑隐藏着不流露出来。我们一家人都有同样的担心。除了布莱恩,大家逐渐接受了虎儿已经死亡这一事实。

每天晚上,布莱恩总要到门口叫虎儿的名字。终于,在邻居通知我们后的第28天,布莱恩的呼唤得到了回答。虎儿从门廊的地板下走了出来。它像往常一样高高地翘着尾巴,表现出一种不同凡响的高傲神态,仿佛从未远离过家门。当它接近大门口时,布莱恩兴奋得连面容都改变了。但无论是布莱恩还是虎儿,都没有在全家人面前表现出公开的亲热。他们只是平静地接受了这一事实,每一个都对另一个的尊严表示尊重。但那天晚上我检查布莱恩的房间时,发现他的脸颊上挂着泪珠,流露出幸福的微笑。虎儿正静静地躺在他弯曲的手臂里,轻轻地打着呼噜。

转眼过去了好几年。如今,虎儿12岁,布莱恩18岁了。布莱恩强烈感到两代人在思想交流方面存在着鸿沟。他正处在自我认识的危机之中。他这种感觉过于强烈,所以他不得不远离家门,和同代人一道去寻找某些问题的答案,而这些答案是在他们父母那里找不到的,部分原因是他们也不知道问题究竟是什么。

Yet, unlike many of his age group, Brian maintained a connection with home. From time to time, at odd hours and without warning, he would appear or call. And always he would ask, "How's my cat? How's Tiger?"

And then one night a call came from a phone booth in downtown Washington. "Brian is sick," an unidentified youth said. "He's asking for you. You'd better come and get him. He's at the 'cave' on P Street."

It was 4:15 a. m. Two hours later following the educated guess of a policeman, I found the "cave". It turned out to be a slum basement, filthy and crowded, where 20 to 30 teenagers slept. Brian was there. He had pneumonia[1].

"Hello, Father," he mumbled. "I blew it again, didn't I? How's Tiger?"

we brought him home to recover, not with all those unanswered questions: Who am I? Why am I here? Where am I going?

---

[1] pneumonia /nju(:)'məunjə/ n. 肺炎

和其他同龄人不同的是,布莱恩常常和家人保持联系。他经常事先不告知,说不定什么时候就突然出现中打来一个电话。他总是要问:"我的猫好吗?虎儿怎么样?"

一天晚上,有人从华盛顿闹市区的一个电话亭打来了电话。"布莱恩病了,"一位不明身份的青年在电话里说,"他要求见你。你最好来把他接回家。他住在P大街的'洞穴'里。"当时是凌晨4点15分。两个小时之后,我根据警察有所根据的猜测,找到了那个"洞穴"。它原来是贫民区里的一间地下室,又脏又挤,有二三十个十几岁的孩子睡在一块。布莱恩也在其中,他患了肺炎。

"你好,爸爸!"他含糊不清地说,"我又搞砸了,不是吗?虎儿好吗?"

我们将他领回家养病,由于布莱恩没有找到那些问题的答案,仍不愿呆在家里。这些问题是:我是谁?我为什么要来到这个世界?我将走向何方?

The next cal, from Philadelphia, came at a more reasonable hour. It was 6:15 p. m., and we were just starting dinner. "Father, can I come home?" Brian asked. "I've been robbed. Of everything. My clothes, my wallet, my guitar, even my poetry. "There was a

catch in his voice. This, I think, was the final blow in a series of hard knocks which persuaded Brian that his search for himself must take a different direction. "Of course you can," I said. The conversation ended on a familiar note: "Tell Tiger I'll be home tomorrow."

So, once again, Brian came home. But again he left. This time it was for good, leaving us his cat while he began to find some answers to adulthood.

Today, married, he visits from time to time. He is making his own life with his new wife—and without Tiger.

我们后来接到的下一个电话是从费城打来的,时间比较合理,是在下午 6 点 15 分。我们刚开始吃晚饭。布莱恩问道:"爸爸,我能回家来吗?我被人抢了,什么都没有给我留下。他们抢走了我的衣服、钱包、吉它,甚至我写的诗歌。"他的声音噎住了。我想这一次该是他一系列严重打击中的最后一次。这些打击足以说服他,使他明白探索自己的道路应该改变方向了。我说:"你当然可以回家。"谈话结束之时,他又重复了一句熟悉的话:"请告诉虎儿,我明天就回家。"

于是,布莱恩又一次回来了,但他随后就又离开了。这一次是一去不回头。他开始寻找关于成年期的答案。但在出发之前,他将猫留给了我们。

如今,他已经结婚成家,不时地回家探望小住。他正和新婚妻子一道开创自己的新生活——但虎儿不在他的身边。

After Brian left home that first time, Gwyn, age 10, took over the responsibility for Tiger's care. Small and slightly scatterbrained[1], she was in love with the animal world and even refused to watch movies or television programs in which animals might get hurt. Gwyn was miserable in school, but we did not know it then, for in some ways she was harder to communicate with than Brian. For her, as for Brian, Tiger became the companion to whom she could pour out her heart and show her love without fear of rejection or ridicule[2]. And she profited[3] from the discipline of maintaining a regular feeding schedule for Tiger and cleaning out his sandbox.

In the late summer before Tiger's 16th year began, Gwyn became increasingly concerned with his health. He was slowing down noticeably, and his hearing and eyesight were failing. One night Gwyn came to me with the inevitable[4] question: "Father, what if Tiger dies? What am I going to do?" And with the question came a flood of tears.

Tiger was stretched out on the floor, is ears pricked, his eyes looking at Gwyn. Then he turned and looked at me, as if to say, "Well, old man, how do you handle this one?"

---

[1] scatterbrained *a.* 注意力不集中的
[2] ridicule /ˈridikjuːl/ *n.* 嘲笑；奚落
[3] profit *vi.* 得益
[4] inevitable /inˈevitəbl/ *a.* 不可避免的；必然的

布莱恩第一次离家之后,格温才 10 岁,她承担了照看虎儿的责任。虽然她个子矮小,有点丢三落四,但对所有动物都十分喜欢。如果电影或电视节目中有动物受伤,她甚至会拒绝观看。格温在学校的生活很痛苦,当时我们并不知道,因为在某些方面她比布莱恩更难和人交流思想。猫对她就跟布莱恩一样,虎儿成了她的伙伴。她可以倾诉衷肠表明她的爱,而不必担心遭到拒绝或嘲笑。她有规律地喂猫和清扫猫粪便箱,从这种训练中受益不浅。

那年夏天,当虎儿将进入 16 岁时,格温日益关注着它的健康。它明显地行动迟缓,听力和视力日益衰退。一天晚上,格温带着那个不可回避的问题找到我说:"爸爸,假如虎儿死了怎么办?那我怎么办呢?"提问之后,她潸然泪下。

虎儿平躺在地上,竖起耳朵,眼睛注视着格温,然后又回过头看看我,好像在说:"嗯,老朋友,你怎么处理这个问题?"

"Gwyn," I began, "everyone must die. And when someone does, those who love him weep, and mourn his death. But when we weep at the death of someone we love, or at the realization that death will soon take him away, aren't we weeping at our own loss?

"Think about it. Do you pity Tiger because he is going to die, or do you feel sorry for yourself because you are going to lose him? Tiger has had a long life—longer than most. He has been loved and cared for. If he could tell you how he wants to be remembered, I think he would say that he wants you to recall the happy times, the joy and comfort that he has brought you, the good lessons that you have learned from him. I think he would want you to remember him with smiles.

"Tiger is going to die, Gwyn. Not tomorrow, maybe, but soon. He will get sick and be in pain. Then you will have to decide: Will Tiger be kept alive, even if he is suffering, just so you can delay losing him for a few days? Or will you ask the vet to end his suffering?"

This time, Gwyn sat quietly, listening to me and not bouncing as she usually did. And Tiger, as I ended my speech, put his head down, closed his eyes and drifted off to sleep.

"格温,"我对她说。"人都是要死的。当某个人死去时,那些爱他的人,就会为他哀悼、哭泣。我们为我们爱的死者哭泣时,或者想到他的死即将使他远离这个世界时,难道不也是为我们自己的损失感到难受吗?

"好好想想吧,你怜悯虎儿是因为它将不久于人世,还是因为你将失去它而为自己感到难受呢?虎儿活得已经够长了——比大多数的猫活得都长。它一直受到疼爱,得到照顾。如果它能够告诉你,它想怎样被你怀念,我想它会说要你回忆过去那些幸福的时刻以及它带给你的快乐和安慰,回忆你从它身上学到的东西。我想它会要你面带微笑地怀念它。

"虎儿将要死去,格温,也许不是明天,但会很快的。它将得病,痛苦万分,那里你要作出决定,是哪怕在虎儿忍受巨大痛苦的情况下,为了使你暂时不失去它而拖延几天让它继续活着,还是请兽医尽快结束它的痛苦呢?"

这一次,格温静坐在那里听我说,没有像往常那样蹦跳起来。我结束谈话时,虎儿低下头闭上眼睛,渐渐进入了梦乡。

When we reached the animal clinic, Gwyn had to carry Tiger inside. For several days he had been unable to keep his food down. He had lost control of his body functions. The flesh had evaporated from his frame, leaving his ribs showing, his hips sharply prominent[1].

At the clinic, the doctor examined Tiger for long, grave moments. "Well, Gwyn," he said finally, "I can keep him here for a few days, feed him on a liquid diet, try to build him up—but I can't make any guarantees[2]. His nerves are breaking down. He can't control himself. It's old age."

Gwyn searched the doctor's carefully neutral face. "I don't want him to suffer," she said. "I want what's best for him."

She picked Tiger up from the examining table, held him tightly to her breast, his head on her shoulder. Her eyes grew moist. Tiger was completely quiet in her arms, as if awaiting her decision.

"I want you to put him to sleep," Gwyn said to the doctor. Her voice broke, and tears spilled down her cheeks. She put Tiger back on the table. Then she turned to me and smiled through her tears.

---

[1] prominent /ˈprɔminənt/ *a.* 显著的；卓越的
[2] guarantee /ˌgærənˈtiː/ *n.* 保证（书）

我们到达兽医诊所之后,格温只能抱着虎儿走了进去。几天来,它一吃东西就会吐出来,大小便失禁,肌肉萎缩,只剩下一个骨架,肋骨和胯骨明显凸起。

在诊所里,医生认真细致地为虎儿作了检查。"格温,"医生最后说,"我可以把它留我这里养几天,给它吃流食,尽力使它强壮起来,但我不能作出任何保证。它的神经系统正在垮掉,它不能自控。它的年龄太大了。"

格温认真地注视着医生面无表情的脸说:"我不想让它忍受痛苦。我要你对采取最不痛苦的措施。"

格温从诊断桌上抱起虎儿,将它紧紧地贴在胸前。虎儿的脑袋依偎在她的肩膀上。她的眼睛湿润了。虎儿静静地躺在她的怀里,好像在等待着她的决定。

"我要你让它安然长眠,"格温对医生说,她的声音哽咽了,眼泪扑簌簌从她的脸颊上滚落下来。随后,她将虎儿放回原处,转向我,透过泪珠勉强露出一丝笑容。

I said nothing. I couldn't. Instead, I put my arm around her shoulders and squeezed. Again she smiled at me through the tears, a shaky smile that told me she was satisfied with her decision. At the door we paused and turned for a last look. Tiger was sitting quietly on the examining table. He looked at us, eyes bright, ears perked. Though weak from hunger, he sat up tall and calmly watched us go.

Gwyn and I got into the car. I put my head down onto the steering wheel and sobbed—the first time I had cried in years. Gwyn sobbed, too. But when I could look at her, she was smiling once again, a glowing look through the tears now drying on her cheeks.

Later that day, after I had called Brian, I wept again. Could I not, I asked myself, accept the advice I had given Gwyn? Did Tiger's loss mean so much? Then the thought came: My tears were not tears of sadness. They represented a number of emotions:

I was proud—of Gwyn and the courage and firmness of her decision.

I was satisfied—With myself, as a father who had been able to give to his youngest child an insight which helped her through an emotional crisis.

And I was grateful—to Tiger, for the contributions[1] he had made in maintaining our communication with, and to Gwyn's maturing.

For a cat, Tiger was a pretty good teacher.

---

[1] contribution /ˌkɔntriˈbjuːʃən/ n. 贡献

我什么也没有说，我什么也说不出来，只得将一只手臂环住她的肩膀，紧紧地抱着她。她噙着热泪又一次向我微笑。她强作笑脸是告诉我，她对自己的决定是满意的。走到门口时，我们停住脚步最后看了虎儿一眼。它正安详地卧在诊断桌上，睁着明亮的眼睛，竖起耳朵，望着我们。尽管它忍受着饥饿折磨的身体无力，但仍卧在那里高兴地抬起脑袋，安静地目送我们离去。

我和格温上了汽车。我将头俯在方向盘上啜泣。这是多年以来第一次哭。格温也在抽泣。当我止住哭声抬眼看她时，她的脸上带着未干的泪痕，目光炯炯有神。又一次露出了笑容。

那天回来给布莱恩挂完电话之后，我又一次落泪了。我扪心自问：难道自己都不能接受那些曾向格温提出的忠告吗？失去虎儿难道意义就如此重大吗？我猛然意识到我的眼泪不再是悲伤的眼泪，而是代表着多种情感。

我为格温感到自豪——她有勇气，果断地作出了决定。

作为父亲，我对自己感到心满意足——我能给予女儿深刻的理解，帮助她度过了感情危机。

我非常感激虎儿，因为它为保持我们和布莱恩之间的感情交流以及格温的长大成熟作出了贡献。

Jumper Back Home

The little black colt[1] was born just before dawn. Miserable and bewildered[2], he lay on the straw and shivered. A large object bent over him, wrapped him in something warm and lifted him. He struggled, but strong arms held him close and a comforting voice spoke to him.

As the colt touched the great, warm body of his mother, his muzzle[3] pushed against her. He opened his mouth and grabbed. Sweet milk trickled[4] down his throat. The mare's dark eyes looked him over tenderly.

The master, a Siberian farmer named Ozerov, stood over him. To the boy beside him, Ozerov said, "Come, Denis, my son, what shall we call him? He is yours, as I promised."

Denis reached out and stroked the silky head. "His legs are long and slender. Let's call him Jumper," he said.

Jumper was intelligent and soon began to repay the tenderness shown him. He tagged after the master and the boy, nuzzling[5] them as if to say: "I am yours. I will do all you ask."

---

[1] colt /kəult/ n. 雄马驹（四岁或五岁以下者）
[2] bewildered /bi'wildə(r)d/ a. 迷惑的；不知所措的
[3] muzzle n. 口鼻部
[4] trickle vi. 滴流
[5] nuzzle vt. 用鼻子爱抚

战马回乡

小黑马驹是在黎明前出生的。它躺在干草堆上,浑身颤抖,一副痛苦而迷惘的神情。一个庞然大物向它俯下身,用某种暖和的东西将它裹住,然后把它举了起来。它竭力挣扎,但那两只强壮的手臂紧紧地抱住它,他听到一种令人安慰的声音对它说话。

小马驹触到妈妈那巨大而温暖的身躯,便用口鼻亲昵地在它身上蹭来蹭去。它张开嘴,噙住妈妈的奶头。甜甜的奶水顺着喉咙流了下来。母马的一双黑眼睛疼爱地看着它。

马的主人是西伯利亚的一位农民,名叫奥泽罗夫。此时,它站在那里俯视着小马驹。他的身旁还站着一个男孩子。过了一会儿,奥泽罗夫对那个男孩说:"丹尼斯,我的儿子,过来。我们给马驹起个什么名字呢?它现在归你了,我早就答应过你的。"

丹尼斯伸出手抚摸小马驹丝绸般光滑的头。"它的腿又细又长。我们就叫它跃跃吧,"丹尼斯说。

跃跃很有灵性,不久便开始回报主人对它的疼爱。它紧紧地跟在主人和那个男孩身后,用鼻子摩擦他们,好像在说:"我是你们的。你们要我做什么,我就做什么。"

When the days grew warm, he and his mother were turned loose with the other horses. A piebald[1] filly[2] attracted him. He sniffed her from her head to the very tip of her tail. Then, joyously, he rose on his hind legs and spun like a top. The filly watched admiringly.

But a chestnut colt came near, baring his teeth. Jumper shrank against the fence, too frightened to make a sound.

"Stop! What's this?" The master's voice sent the reddish-brown colt fleeing.

"Well, Jumper, you gave yourself a scare! A little too smart, maybe?" The man stroked him. All was again as it should be.

"He's going to be a fine horse, Denis," the old man said. "Horses are like people—good and bad. Take the chestnut—he's ill-tempered and a coward. He'll do well enough for hard work on the farm. But we'll train Jumper slowly, with kindness."

The master stroked[3] Jumper. From a distance, the chestnut colt watched them." Just you wait!" his dark look threatened.

One morning that summer the master led Jumper to the stable and locked him in without his mother. Puzzled, he raced back and forth, whinnying[4].

---

[1] piebald /'paibɔːld/ *a.* 花斑的
[2] filly *n.* 小雌马（通常未满四岁）
[3] stroke *vt.* 抚摸
[4] whinny /'(h)wini/ *vi.* 马嘶

天气变暖时，主人将跃跃和它妈妈以及别的马的缰绳一起松开，让汤米在草地自由玩耍。一匹黑白花斑的小母马吸引了跃跃的视线。它从头到尾细细地闻了一遍小母马，然后欢快地举起两条前腿站起来，像陀螺一样打起转来。小母马在一旁赞佩地注视着它。

但就在这时，一匹雄性的小红棕马凑了过来，龇牙咧嘴的，露出一副凶相。跃跃被吓得不敢出声，退缩到了篱笆前面。

"站住！怎么回事？"听到主人的呵斥声，小红棕马赶紧逃之夭夭。

"喂，跃跃，你怎么自己吓自己！也许有点聪明过头了吧？"奥泽罗夫轻轻地抚摸着它。一切又恢复了原样。

"丹尼斯，它会成为一匹好马的，"奥泽罗夫说，"马也和人一样有好有坏。就拿那匹红棕马来说吧，它脾气坏，又是个胆小鬼，只能让它呆在农场干干力气活儿。但对跃跃，我们要慢慢地训练它，耐心地训练它。"

奥泽罗夫轻轻地抚摸着跃跃。那匹小红棕马在远处盯着他们。它阴森的目光好像在威胁着说："你们等着瞧吧！"

那年夏天的一个早上，奥泽罗夫将跃跃牵到马厩里锁起来，把它和妈妈牵去分隔开来了。跃跃感到莫名其妙，便嘶叫着在马厩里来回奔跑。

For days he made the air ring with his calls. One morning, he heard grief-stricken neighs[1] from the next stable. It was the voice of the piebald filly. Jumper sensed that she, too, had been separated from her mother. Plunging about in his stall, he demanded to be set free.

At last the master came. "Hey, what's all the fuss? You think your friend is in trouble and you can comfort her? Well, maybe you can." Eagerly, Jumper followed the master into the yard and dashed to the filly, whom Denis was leading from her stall. They greeted each other with sniffs and little whinnies. So it was that Jumper made himself the filly's protector.

A day came when all the colts were turned into a meadow together. The chestnut, showing his ugly temper, cornered Jumper. At that instant something happened to the black colt. A ball of fire seemed to gather within him and run along every nerve of his body. He turned and let fly with both hind legs. Before the chestnut had time to recover, Jumper faced him and plunged forward. To his amazement, the chestnut fled.

Now Jumper felt strong and fearless, looking to no one for protection. The sense of power was glorious, but it did not mean that he was independent. His need of human beings was as real as his need of the sun.

---

[1] neigh /nei/ *vi.* 马嘶

一连好几天,它的嘶叫声响得震天动地似的。但突然有一天清早,它听到隔壁马厩里传来悲哀的马叫声。是那匹黑白花斑的小母马的叫声。跃跃意识到它也和妈妈分开了。它在马厩里乱踢乱撞起来,要求放它出去。

奥泽罗夫终于来了。"喂,闹腾什么呀?是不是你认为你的朋友有了难,你要去安慰它?那好吧,也许你能安慰它。"跃跃急不可待地跟着主人进了院子,向母马厩奔去。这时,丹尼斯正好将它从马厩里牵了出来。它们相互闻了闻,轻轻地嘶叫了几声,算是打过了招呼。就这样,跃跃便成了这匹小母马的"护花使者"。

一天,所有的小马驹都被赶到了同一块草地上。那匹小红棕马又要坏脾气了。它将跃跃逼到了没有退路的地方。就在这一刹那间,跃跃身上突然发生了某种奇异的变化,它的体内好像突然聚集了一个火球,这个火球正沿着每一根神经滚动。它转过身,用两条后腿猛踢过去。红棕马还没反应过来,跃跃便又转身面对着它冲过去。出乎意料的是,红棕马立刻吓得落荒而逃。

现在,跃跃感到自己非常强壮,而且无所畏惧,不指再需要任何人的保护了。强壮的感觉的确十分令人愉快,但这并不意味着它已经独立了。它仍然确实需要人类,就像它确实需要阳光一样。

Before he was two years old, Jumper had learned to carry a rider and to draw a light sleigh[1]. He knew that he was the best pupil among the colts, and the knowledge made him proud.

One day in 1914, the church bell began to ring, slowly and solemnly. War had been declared! Army officers arrived in the village to inspect the horses. One of them opened Jumper's mouth wide to look at his teeth.

When the man had gone, the master put both arms around Jumper's neck and laid his face sadly against the glossy coat. Denis wailed, "Oh, Jumper! You are going away to war and we'll never see you again."

A few days later, Ozerov's best horses, Jumper among them, were taken to the railroad station. There, they were made to go up the runway into a car. The train moved off.

On the long trap west Jumper learned for the first time what it was to be afraid of human beings. Once, when one of them brought him food, he whinnied a greeting. The man seized a broom and brought it down on his head.

---

[1] sleigh /sleɪ/ n. 雪橇

跃跃不到两岁就学会了载人和拉较轻的雪车。它知道自己是小马驹中学得最好的一个，这一点使它非常自豪。

1914年的一天，教堂开始响起了钟声，缓慢而严肃的钟声。宣战了！军官们纷纷来到村里挑选马匹。其中一位军官看中了跃跃，他掰开了跃跃的嘴，看了看它的牙齿。

这位军官走了之后，奥泽罗夫伸出双臂搂住跃跃的脖子，伤心地将脸贴着它那光滑的皮毛。丹尼斯哭着叫道："噢，跃跃！你就要去打仗了，我们再也见不到你了。"

几天之后，奥泽罗夫最好的几匹马——其中包括跃跃——都被牵到了火车站。然后，它们穿过一条通道，走进了火车车厢。火车开走了。

在西去的漫长旅途中，跃跃第一次懂得了害怕人是一种什么感觉。有一次，一个人拿来草料给它吃，它嘶叫了一声表示欢迎。谁知那人操起一把扫帚就朝它劈头盖脸地打了下来。

One day Jumper heard a man repeated his name. "Jumper...Jumper!" Jumper stretched his neck and was tenderly stroked. The man, a top sergeant, was in charge of the horse train. He had lists of the horses' names. Coming from a Russian village, he understood animals. Jumper's friendliness and intelligence appealed to[1] him.

Somewhere on that journey, the sergeant bought a notebook and wrote on its cover: "Personal Service Record of the Siberian Colt Jumper." On the first page he wrote: "To anyone who may find this book, be it known that it is the record of Jumper, a very gentle Jumper. I beg anyone into whose hands the horse and this notebook may fall to continue the record of his experience in the service of our country."

Months later, Jumper found himself on a field where a fierce battle was raging[2]. Sparks flared, and tongues of flame split the dust. Heavy smoke hung in the air. Jumper hardly looked like the same animal that had gone off to war. His ribs showed through his skin and his head hung low.

Through hardships and suffering he had gained an understanding of his new master, Lieutenant Radov. Training had taught him to be calm no matter what happened. And all his senses had been sharpened to detect[3] danger.

---

[1] appeal /əˈpiːl/ to 有吸引力；求助于
[2] rage *vt.* 猛烈进行
[3] detect /dɪˈtekt/ *vt.* 察觉

有一天，跃跃听到一个人一遍又一遍地喊它的名字："跃跃……跃跃！"跃跃伸出脖子。那人爱抚地拍了拍它。这人是一名上士，负责掌管这列运马的火车。他有火车上所有马的花名册。他来自俄国农村，所以很了解动物的习性。他很喜欢跃跃的机智和对人类的友好态度。

上士在旅途中的某个地方买了一个笔记本。他在封面上写道："西伯利亚小马跃跃的服役记录。"随后，他又在第一页上写道："任何发现这个笔记本的人请注意：这是跃跃这匹性情温和的小马的服役记录。我恳请凡是得到这匹马和这个笔记本，请你们继续将它为国效忠的事迹记录下来。"

数月之后，跃跃发现自己来到了正在激战中的战场上。战争已经进入了白热化阶段，火星四溅，火舌乱吐，尘土飞扬，硝烟弥漫。现在，跃跃看上去已经不再像刚到战场时的那副模样了，它的头耷拉着，透过皮肤都能看到它的根根肋骨。

经历了许多的艰苦与磨难之后，它对自己的新主人拉多夫中尉有了一定的了解。它所受到的训练使它明白了，无论发生什么事都要保持镇定。它的全部知觉都敏锐了起来，它能察觉出危险。

Jumper turned his head to his master, who comforted him with caresses. "Jumper," said the lieutenant, "you're a hero. It is you who saved us all today. You sensed the enemy and disobeyed me when I wanted you to ford the stream. You kept us from being caught in a trap. But we're in a bad way, old fellow. The enemy is surrounding us."

That night they retreated. All the next day they were under heavy fire. Suddenly a shell exploded near Jumper, tossing him into the air.

When Jumper came to, he jumped up quickly, though in great pain. Lieutenant Radov lay a few feet away. Jumper waited for him to get into the saddle. But instead men carried the lieutenant away on a stretcher. Jumper followed, leaving a trail[1] of blood.

When Jumper had recovered, World War I was over.

Two years passed. Over the Russian countryside a train rushed eastward loaded with soldiers bound for Siberia. In a corner two young officers were talking in low voices.

Captain Malechek, a cavalryman[2], was discussing horse. "I'm not saying a horse has a mind like a human being," he said, "but it has an amazing understanding. Here's something I'd like to show you." He handed over to Lieutenant Kolosov a stained notebook.

---

[1] trail n. 痕迹
[2] cavalryman /ˈkævəlrimən/ n. 骑兵；地面机械化部队

跃跃将头转向主人，主人爱抚地安慰它说："跃跃，你是个英雄。是你救了我们大家。今天，我刚要骑着你过那条溪流时，你发现了敌情，于是你没有服从我的命令，没让我过那条小溪。你使我们没有落入敌人的圈套。不过，老伙计，我们现在的处境不妙。敌人正在向我们包围过来。"

那天晚上，他们撤退了。第二天，他们一整天都受到敌人猛烈炮火的袭击。突然，一枚炮弹在跃跃附近爆炸，将它掀到了空中。

跃跃一苏醒过来，就立刻忍着巨大的疼痛跳了起来。拉多夫中尉躺在离它不远的地方。跃跃走过去，等待他跨上马鞍。但中尉没有上马，人们用担架把他抬走了。跃跃跟在担架后面，留下了一路血迹。

当跃跃身体康复时，第一次世界大战结束了。

转眼两年过去了。一列向东开往西伯利亚的火车满载着回乡军人飞驰在俄国乡间。火车上，两位年轻军官在一个角落低声交谈。

骑兵上尉马勒切克谈到了马。"我倒不是说马也像人一样有头脑，"他说，"但马的确非常懂事。我来给你看一样东西。"说着，他将一个污迹斑斑的笔记本递给了他的同伴科洛索夫中尉。

"It was written by soldiers unknown to me. It's the service record of a Siberian[1] horse named Jumper, aboard this train. He's not much to look at, but there's something about his eyes. Perhaps the most unusual thing about him is that all these men took the trouble to write about him as if he were a friend."

Lieutenant Kolosov opened the notebook, and read,

"We are on the eve of defeat. I am writing of my faithful friend Jumper. If he survives me, I ask that this notebook go with him...This horse is happy when his master is happy and unhappy when he is sad. His eyes follow every move I make. Treat him as you would a human being...

—Lieutenant Radov."

Kolosov, deeply moved, asked, "What do you plan to do with the horse now?"

"I have my own horse," the captain answered. "You love horses. Take him. It is fitting that you two Siberians be together."

When the train stopped, Jumper was led out of a boxcar. Lieutenant Kolosov patted him on the neck and said tenderly, "Jumper, I know you will serve me faithfully." The familiar Siberian accent delighted Jumper. He turned toward the man with a welcoming whinny.

---

[1] Siberian /sai'biəriən/ *a.* 西伯利亚的

"这是一些我不认识的军人写的。上面记载着一匹名叫跃跃的西伯利亚马在军队中服役的事迹。这匹马现在就在这列火车上。它看上去没有什么特别的地方,但它的两只眼睛却充满了灵性。而对于这匹马来说,也许最不寻常的就是,所有这些军人都不厌其烦地记下了关于它的故事,好像它是一个朋友似的。"

科洛索夫中尉翻开笔记本,读了起来:

"我们就要被打败了。我在这里记录下我忠实的朋友跃跃的事迹。如果我死了,而它仍能活下去,我请求以后接管它的人将这个笔记本随它一起带走……这匹马会因主人的欢乐而欢乐,因主人的忧伤而忧伤。它的目光总是时追随着我的一举一动。请像对待人一样对待它……

——拉多夫中尉"

科洛索夫中尉深深地感动了,他问道:"你现在打算怎样处理这匹马?"

"我自己有马,"上尉回答说,"你喜欢马,你就把它牵走吧。你们俩都是西伯利亚来的,一定会相处得很好的。"

火车到站时,跃跃被牵出了车厢。科洛索夫中尉在马脖子上轻轻地拍了拍,温和地说:"跃跃,我知道你会为我忠心效力的。"听到这熟悉的西伯利亚口音,跃跃非常高兴。它转过头对着这个人,长长地嘶叫了一声表示欢迎。

Once, Jumper had traveled west to fight in a war. Now with this master he was returning east to Lake Baikal. Here Russian troops were gathering to face an enemy in the Far East.

The march was made in snow and bitter cold. One morning Jumper was astonished to find ice under his hoofs. It reminded him of something. He snorted[1].

"What is frightening you, Jumper?" The master asked. Jumper turned his head around as if to say, "It is not fear, but this ice and this countryside. I have been here before."

Next day they came into a village where the soldiers were warmly welcomed. Jumper was put into a good stable, but he was restless. Left alone, he kept inspecting a smelling everything around him.

Suddenly he raised his head and listened. Footsteps approached youthful voice called, "Jumper!"

The door opened. A tall man and a lanky[2] boy came in. By the light of their lantern they looked at the brand on the horse's flank. "Jumper...Jumper!" they cried. "It really is you. Welcome home!"

Next morning the village was excited by the news that Jumper had come back to Ozerov. Everyone hurried to see for himself. It was agreed that this was a miracle!

---

[1] snort *vi.* 喷鼻息
[2] lanky /ˈlæŋki/ *a.* 瘦长的

跃跃曾参加过西线的战役。如今，它要和这位主人回东边的贝加尔湖了。俄国军队正在这里集结，准备对付远东的敌人。

行军途中，地上已经积了雪，天气十分寒冷。一天清早，跃跃惊奇地发现蹄子下面有冰。这使它想起了一些事。它喷了喷响鼻。

"跃跃，什么东西让你害怕了？"主人问道。跃跃转过头，好像在说："我没有害怕，而是这冰和田野让我有些感慨。我以前曾在这里生活过。"

第二天，他们来到一个村庄。在这里，军人们受到了热烈的欢迎。跃跃被安置在一个挺不错的马厩里，但它却躁动不安。当它单独呆在马厩里时，它不停地打量着和闻着周围的东西。

它突然抬起头来，侧耳倾听。他听到了脚步声，有人正朝它走来。随后，他听到一个年轻的声音叫道："跃跃！"

门开了。一个高大的男人和一个身体细长的男孩走了进来。借着手中灯笼的光亮，他们看到了跃跃胁腹上的那个烙印。"跃跃……跃跃！"他们大声喊道，"真的是你。欢迎你回家来！"

第二天早上，全村人都为跃跃又回到了奥泽罗夫身边而激动不已。每个人都赶过来亲眼看看它。大家一致认为，这是一个奇迹。

The din of voices stopped as Ozerov addressed the officer. "Comrade Commander, Jumper is our horse, born in that little stable. The piebald filly over there is his friend. Let me take off his bridle and you'll see that he will go straight to her. Have pity on him and let him stay."

The officer took off the bridle. Jumper tossed his head and ran to join the piebald filly in the corral farthest away.

The officer smiled at Denis, then turned to Ozerov and winked. "I have no right to discharge a good horse, but I have noticed that Jumper is ailing[1]. A sick horse is useless in war. So if you will give a healthy horse in exchange, I'll call it a deal."

Denis and his father cried and laughed. The villagers shouted and shook the officer's hand.

Next morning, everyone turned out to see the soldiers off. Only Jumper seemed worried. Why was he not saddled?

"Good-bye, old comrade," Lieutenant Kolosov whispered in his ear. "I'm sorry to leave you, but you will be happy here." He patted Jumper, vaulted onto another horse and rode off without looking back.

Then Jumper heard the piebald filly neigh. His answer comforted her. He seemed to say. "Don't worry. I'm never going away again!"

---

[1] ail *vi.* 生病

奥泽罗夫对科洛索夫中尉说话时，大家安静了下来。"指挥员同志，跃跃是我们的马，它就出生在那个小马厩里。那边那匹黑白花斑的母马是它的朋友。如果把它的辔鞍拿下来，你会看到它将立刻朝她走去。可怜可怜它，让它留下来吧。"

科洛索夫中尉将辔鞍拿了下来。跃跃头一甩，飞快地跑去和站在围栏最远处的黑白花斑母马相会了。

科洛索夫中尉冲丹尼斯笑了笑，随后转身对奥泽罗夫挤了一下眼睛，说："我无权让一匹身体健康的马退役，但我注意到跃跃病了。病马在战场上是没有用的。因此，如果你愿意用一匹健康的马来与它交换的话，那我们就算成交了。"

丹尼斯和他父亲激动得又是哭又是笑。村民们兴奋地握住了科洛索夫中尉的手，大声欢呼着。

第二天早上，大家都出来为军人们送行。只有跃跃好像满腹心事的样子：为什么不给它套上马鞍呢？

"再见了，老伙计，"科洛索夫中尉冲着跃跃的耳朵小声说。"离开你，我很难过，但你在这里会很快活的。"他轻轻拍了拍跃跃，然后跨上另一匹马，头也不回地走了。

这时，跃跃听到那匹黑白花斑的小母马的嘶叫声。它回了一声，让小母马放心。它仿佛在说："别担心。我再也不走了！"

The old man and Denis, the filly, the farm noises that were music to his ears—all were part of him. It was as if he had never been away. This was his home, beloved and real.

　　奥泽罗夫、丹尼斯和小母马,以及在它听来那么悦耳的农场的喧闹声——所有这些都是它生活的一部分。它觉得自己好像从来没有远离过这里。这是它的家,可爱而又真实的家。

参 考 文 献

1. Big Sky Journal

2. Flying Horse Journal

3. National Geographic Magazine

4. Story Quarterly

5. Short Stories for ESL Students

注：本书有部分资料及图片未能联系到相应作者，请上述作者在看到本书后与本书编著人员及出版社联系，以便我们能够及时支付相应稿酬。